Spiritual

MW00949001

Volume 1

The Gifts, Grace and Flow

of the Holy Spirit

Jan Coverstone

Jan Coverstone

Spiritual Truth Series

Volume 1: The Gifts, Grace and Flow of the Holy Spirit

By Jan Coverstone

Copyright 2017 by Jan Coverstone

Published by JC Life Books Columbia City, Indiana USA

by Createspace

www.jancoverstone.com

ISBN:978-1-54805-611-7

Religion / Christian Life / Spiritual Growth

Discover other books by Jan Coverstone

Let the Living Waters Flow

How You Think Determines Who You Are

Spiritual Warfare: Understanding Biblical Truth & Satan's Deceptions

The Spiritual Truth Series

Volume 1

The Gifts, Grace and Flow of the Holy Spirit

Table of Contents

Chapter 1 - Personal Experience

Chapter 2 - The Promise of the Spirit

Chapter 3 - The Baptism in the Holy Spirit

Chapter 4 - Reasons to Pray in Tongues

Chapter 5 - The Trinity Gives Gifts

Chapter 6 - Vocal Gifts

Chapter 7 - Ministry of Tongues

Chapter 8 - The Interpretation of Tongues

Chapter 9 - All May Prophesy

Chapter 10 - Prophecy

Chapter 11 - Revelation Gifts

Chapter 12 - Power Gifts

Chapter 13 - Led by the Spirit

Chapter 14 - Led by the Spirit: Dreams and Visions

Chapter 15 - Love

Chapter 16 - But Ye Shall Receive Power...

Chapter 17 - The Church and "The Church"

Jan Coverstone

Foreword

Please do not read this book

Please do not read this book if you are just looking for a book to read. However, if you have a desire to learn more about the spiritual gifts and the grace and flow of the Holy Spirit then this book will help you on your journey. The movement of the Holy Spirit is vital to the health of the church and the church is made of people who should know how to walk in the Spirit and be sensitive to His desire. As Paul wrote to the Ephesians that the God of our Lord Jesus Christ, the Father of Glory, may give to you the spirit of wisdom and revelation in the knowledge of Him, the eyes of your understanding being enlightened; that you may know what is the hope of His calling, what are the riches of the glory of His inheritance in the saints, and what is the exceeding greatness of His power toward us who believe according to the working of His mighty power. To have a spirit of wisdom and revelation; to have the eyes of our understanding enlightened; to know the exceeding greatness of His power toward us by the working of His mighty power should be normal.

Normal, nor'mal, a, According to a rule, conforming with a certain type or standard; regular. (New Webster's Dictionary 1991 edition)

The church as the body of Christ and we as individuals should strive to be normal. We should strive to conform to the rule of the Word of God with the standards set forth for us to follow. To do so is normal; it should be the standard by which we live. I pray this book helps on your journey to become normal.

Jan Coverstone

Preface

The Holy Spirit was promised to be a comforter; one who walks with us, helps us and indwells our being. The Holy Spirit draws us to Christ both before and after salvation. I present this first volume in the Spiritual Truth Series on the Holy Spirit as a result of study and my personal experiences. I have learned and taught about the Holy Spirit and His ministry at Christian Training Center and Christian Fellowship Church. I am a charismatic or Pentecostal and believe in the beautiful gift of tongues both for personal and corporate use. I also believe all the spirituals Paul wrote about in First Corinthians chapters twelve to fourteen should have a vital, dynamic presence and function in the body of Christ.

I have been alarmed, astonished and amazed by many charismatic or Pentecostal believers who really do not understand the importance of tongues and prophecy. I have also found few who know what the Bible teaches and could defend their position from the Bible. Those are addressed in this volume. It is written as a teaching manual along with a workbook to inform, inspire and improve the lives of those who read and study this volume. To welcome the Holy Spirit into our lives in a deeper, more meaningful, and more powerful way begins not only by understanding the gifts or spirituals He presents but also learning how the Holy Spirit flows and the grace with which the Holy Spirit leads us. It is not enough to know of the gifts the Holy Spirit bestows but to know also how they function in our lives in a very real and practical manner.

Jan Coverstone

Chapter One: Personal Experience

I said I will never follow God in my lifetime; I will die first. God knew the foolishness of my statement and by His grace intervened in my life. He did, however let me come very close. There were three of us who decided to partake in a variety of drugs while sitting in my '57 Chevy. I started feeling strange, not strange because of the drugs but I realized if I didn't think about breathing I didn't breathe. Then my vision went haywire and looked as though I was watching an old black and white television with bad reception and a lot of snow on the screen. I asked one fellow to check my pulse; I was having trouble breathing. The other guy dove out through the open window and left. I sensed a presence standing outside the driver's door and heard or felt an impression in my mind which stated: "You need to ask God for help". I didn't feel I was in a position to argue so I said, "God you get me through this and I will try and follow you." It took several hours for my vision to return enough to drive. That was the beginning of my journey.

I didn't have a lot of church experience. I attended some youth activities at a Free Methodist Church where my grandmother's brother was the pastor. Along with my brother and sister we would spend a week or so with my mom's sister to attend vacation bible school. I don't remember much from either experience but through my younger years I sensed God was real and talked to Him. I don't remember how much He responded to me and why I reached a point where I believed and vocalized the opening statement of this chapter. I had started living on my own between my junior and senior year of high school. I had begun training in martial arts the week I graduated. I was not friendly and had built cold hard walls around myself. Training was an outlet; I pushed myself extremely hard not caring if I lived through what I was doing. I didn't like very many people and had little respect for everyone else. I am not even sure how much I liked or respected myself.

After the experience in my '57 Chevy life went on. I really didn't know anything about following God and probably did a poor job of trying to follow. I was with a friend in a park and started wondering what the world would be like without human intervention. What beauty would the world have? How would things be different? Questions bounced around in my mind but no answers were apparent at this time.

The questions raced through my mind as I went to work which at that time was on third shift in a plating factory. There were only two of us scheduled to work on that shift and the other person didn't show so I was working alone. My mind was trying to work through all the questions dancing in my head. Finally, sometime during the early part of the night my thoughts went in this direction. If God is real then He created this earth and everything else. If God is real then the Bible is probably true. If God is real and He created all things and if the Bible is true then God is the creator of life. If I want to know the answers to life and the questions about life then maybe I should ask the creator of life. What a novel idea. If God was real and if the Bible is true then I should ask God to answer my questions about life because He created life.

"Okay God, if you are real I want to know. When I reach up my right hand let me feel the warmth of your bosom that I may gather strength from that." Warmth of your bosom; where did that come from? I don't remember the last time I used the word bosom. A little voice inside me said, "Lift up your hand". I can't do this work with one hand up in the air. "Lift up your hand." If someone comes in they will think I am crazy trying to work with one hand up in the air. "Just lift your hand". I started lifting my right hand slowly looking around to see if anyone would come into the factory and see me in the middle of the night. When I reached above my head it felt like my hand was six or eight inches above the flame on a gas stove. I looked at my hand and thought maybe I should never wash my hand—I touched the warmth of God. My second thought was my hand would be very dirty in less than a week so that probably was not a good idea.

I was standing on a boardwalk maybe a foot or eighteen inches off the floor and looked to my right and there was a yellowish, bright crystalline haze moving through the factory. I thought that is unusual I have never seen that before. The haze continued to waft around the factory and I really do not remember when it disappeared. I started asking God a lot of questions and heard a booming voice come from the upper rafters. There was a small storage place over the one portion of the factory and I went up to see if someone had wired a speaker up there just to play a joke on me. I could tell by the dust on the floor there were no footprints so no one was playing a joke on me.

I resumed working and asking God questions. The voice answered; the voice of God. For most of the night we carried on a conversation and He answered my questions not only about life but about special aspects of life. I asked a question about the martial arts and He answered. It seemed so natural and effortless like that is how it should be. I ask God questions and He answers the questions in an audible voice. It was a great night and I was bursting with excitement so I went to talk to my mom and dad. They had started attending church sometime during my senior year in high school. After telling all the events of the previous night my dad said; "you are saved'. I said that is nice what does that mean? That is when you accept Jesus and now you should go to church. I had not been to church since the time I had went on a Mother's day a year or two before because that was what mom said she wanted. I decided to attend their church the next day.

I went to my parent's house the next morning and my sister opened the door. I was smiling (people used to ask me if I ever smiled and I could never remember the last time I had smiled) and said; "Want to go to church with me?" Her mouth dropped open and she looked at me for a moment then decided she would go with me. Mom and Dad went to the Bible school lesson and I drank coffee and waited for my sister. We arrived before the Sunday school class was over and stood and talked quietly for a few minutes. The church used folding metal chairs set in rows so we sat to the left side with my dad on the far left, my sister sat between dad and mom; I sat on my mom's right side. We were singing a song about victory in Jesus when my sister started to cry and arose to go up front. Dad took his right hand and took hold of her left hand. Mom took her left hand and grabbed my sister's right hand and reached her right hand behind her and held out her ring finger and little finger and wiggled them to me. I grabbed those two fingers with my left hand and then decided I didn't want to go to the front as I didn't understand what was happening.

I tried to let loose of her hand but my hand decided not to cooperate. I thought this is strange, my hand will not open. I felt two hands, one on each side of my ribcage smack my ribs and lift me from my chair. Ok, I

3

guess I will go to the front. I had my encounter with God on Friday night and this was Sunday morning. I had not grown in the grace of God so it only took a few steps to think that wasn't very nice of that guy to lift me from my chair. A couple more steps gave me the determination to see who it was so I could tell him after church that if he ever touched me again there would be consequences. I looked to where we were seated and there is no one around. I thought oh well maybe that is what happens when you go to church. My sister kneeled down and I thought oh so that is what you do when you go up front. I knelt down also. I prayed and asked God to help me help others to find Him. I also reminded Him my sister was crying and asked if He was going to do anything about it. I had no idea how to pray and what to say so I repeated the simple prayer about helping others and reminded Him again my sister was still crying and it was starting to bug me and it was probably bothering others also. This kept repeating until I became frustrated and didn't want to continue saying the same prayer but could not think of anything else to say.

I heard someone say; "let's lay him down." I thought, great now they are laying people down in front of the church. I felt my body being moved and realized, oh, they were talking about me. When I was flat on my back I was gone. I remember nothing about what happened or how long I was lying there. I heard the voice of God saying "I am going to lift you up." I became aware of my mom on her knees sitting on her heels and praying in an unknown language. I knew it was my mom's voice but didn't know the language. I became aware of another woman on my left on her knees sitting on her heels praying in a different yet unknown language. I was lying flat on my back and my mom and another woman had my arms straight up from my chest. I wondered what God meant when He said he would lift me up. Lift me up in the community; lift me up in a church somewhere; I felt my back come off the floor, oh, he was just going to lift me off the floor. I remember feeling a strain in my lower back because, neither my mom nor the other woman, were going to release their grips on my arm until after they were lifted to their feet and I was lifted higher than their outstretched arms.

My legs did not bend and I made no effort to arise from the prone position. I was lifted straight to a standing position with my feet being about eighteen inches to two feet above the floor. I remained there for a moment and was gently set on my feet. When my feet touched the floor I began speaking in another language and jumping around. I do not remember how the service ended, but I went to my parent's house to visit and ask questions. I said that was an interesting service; what happened? Does the Bible talk about this funny language? Dad took his bible and showed me passages on tongues and gave some explanation of how it is to be used and how it functions. My Spiritual journey and my relationship with a loving Father had an explosive beginning. I have wondered why. Why is my experience different than others? What was the purpose of the way events unfolded? I have often wondered how it impacted the other sixty to seventy people who were at the service that day. It was just what God did; I was the recipient of His doing. I have no other explanation.

I was excited, thrilled and eager to share with others about what happened to me. Not everyone was excited or believed and most didn't want to hear about a funny language. It was so real and vital to me I had to know more and searched for books and elder Christians to give insight. I remember one man who I had attended school with took me to his grandmother's house so she could argue me straight about tongues. It didn't work; I believe in the value of tongues and the benefits of the practice more than ever. The experience of receiving the baptism of the Holy Spirit convinced me beyond a shadow of a doubt the experience was and is real for all who open themselves to the Lord. It was the acceptable norm for the early church and should be the norm for the church today. The Holy Spirit is dynamic and His interaction with the church should also be dynamic. The Holy Spirit is a gentleman and never does anything outside the character and love of the Trinity. This series will focus on the dunamis, the dynamic, and the dynamite of the Holy Spirit's power and give insights as to how to listen and flow with the Holy Spirit.

Chapter Review

God allows us to make our own choices. Our acceptance of Him as Lord and Savior is only decided by ourselves. Often times a near death experience is the motivation we require to make that choice. Sadly some never get the last minute chance to make that decision.

Everyone's personal experience with God is unique to them. Mine was extreme and unusual to most people; to the point of disbelief for many. I can only explain it by saying this must have been what it took to get my attention and show me things that God would need me to know on my journey through life and in my mission for him.

I have had people say things like "If I had that experience maybe I would understand better." Apparently God disagrees or we might all have similar experiences. I do know I am not the only one to experience God in unique ways. I would assume you are not as stubborn as I and there are experiences I have had which you would not desire to have. I do realize from mine and other's experiences that God is alive and all powerful and does desire to have a relationship with us and can do miraculous things to facilitate it. And the Holy Spirit is still sent to be an active part of our lives.

Chapter Two: The Promise of the Spirit

Few would argue against the Holy Spirit's working in the church and world. Disagreements occur over how He works and even to the extent of His working in the life of a believer. That He does work is not in question, but are the New Testament experiences of the early church not only valid, but useful and proper for the body of Christ today? Yes, I believe they are vital and necessary, but I do not stand alone in this belief. I stand with millions of believers. We believe the Bible is the Word of God so we will highlight some references to the Holy Spirit from the Bible.

I indeed baptize you with water unto repentance, but He who is coming after me is mightier than I, whose sandals I am not worthy to carry. He will baptize you with the Holy Spirit and fire. (Mt. 3:11)

And he preached, saying, "*There comes One after me who is mightier than I, whose sandal strap I am not worthy to stoop down and loose. I indeed baptize you with water, but He will baptize you with the Holy Spirit. (Mk. 1:7-8) John answered, saying to all, "I indeed baptize you with water, but one mightier than I is coming, whose sandal strap I am not worthy to loose. He will baptize you with the Holy Spirit and with fire.* (Lk 3:16)

And John bore witness, saying, "*I saw the Spirit descending from heaven like a dove and He remained upon Him. I did not know Him, but He who sent me to baptize with water said to me, 'Upon whom you see the Spirit descending, and remaining on Him, this is He who baptizes with the Holy Spirit.' And I have seen and testified that this is the Son of God*." (Jn. 1:23-24)

All the gospels record the words of John the Baptist saying Jesus would baptize you with the Holy Spirit. This is a point worth remembering and we will return and have further exposition on this concept: Jesus is the one who baptizes with the Holy Spirit. The Holy Spirit baptizes us into the body of Christ and our bodies are baptized into water. Recognizing this distinction allows for a greater understanding and less confusion on who baptizes and what are the differences.

"If a son asks for bread from any father among you will he give him a stone? Or if he asks for a fish, will be give him a serpent instead of a

fish? Or if he asks for an egg, will he offer him a scorpion? If you then, being evil, know how to give good gifts to your children, how much more will your heavenly Father give the Holy Spirit to those who ask Him!" (Lk 11:11-13)

"On the last day, that great day of the feast, Jesus stood and cried out. Saying, "If anyone thirsts let him come to Me and drink. He who believes in Me, as the Scripture has said, out of his heart will flow rivers of living water." But this He spoke concerning the Spirit whom those believing in Him would receive; for the Holy Spirit was not yet given because Jesus was not yet glorified. (Jn. 7:37-39)

"And I will pray the Father and He will give you another Helper, that He may abide with you forever—The Spirit of truth, whom the world cannot receive, because it neither sees Him nor knows Him; but you know Him, for He dwells with you and will be in you. (Jn. 14:16-17) *But the Helper, the Holy Spirit whom the Father will send in My name, He will teach you all things, and bring to your remembrance all things that I said to you.* (Jn. 14:26)

"Behold. I send the Promise of My Father upon you; but tarry in the city of Jerusalem until you are endued with power from on high." (Lk.24:49

And being assembled together with them, He commanded them not to depart from Jerusalem, but to wait for Promise of the Father, "which," He said, "you have heard from Me; for John truly baptized with water, but you shall be baptized with the Holy Spirit not many days from now." Therefore, when they had come together, they asked Him, saying, "Lord, will You at this time restore the kingdom to Israel?" And He said to them, "It is not for you to know times or seasons which the Father has put in His own Authority. But you shall receive power when the Holy Spirit has come upon you; and you shall be witnesses to Me in Jerusalem, and in all Judea and Samaria, and to the end of the earth." (Acts. 1:4-8)

When the day of Pentecost had fully come, they were all with one accord in one place. And suddenly there came a sound from heaven, as of a rushing mighty wind, and it filled the whole house where they were sitting. Then there appeared to them divided tongues, as of fire, and one sat upon each of them. And they were all filled with the Holy Spirit and began to speak with other tongues, as the Spirit gave them utterance. (Acts 2:1-4)

But Peter, standing up with the eleven, raised his voice and said to them, "Men of Judea and all who dwell in Jerusalem, let this be known to you, and heed my words. For these are not drunk, as you suppose, since it is only the third hour of the day. But this is what was spoken by the prophet Joel: And it shall come to pass in the last days, says God, That I will pour out My Spirit on all flesh; your sons and daughters shall prophesy, your young men shall see visions, your old men shall dream dreams, And on My menservants and on My maidservants I will pour out My Spirit in those days; and they shall prophesy. (Acts 2:14-18)

Not only did John the Baptist talk about Christ being the one who baptizes with or into the Holy Spirit but Christ Himself said it was the Promise of the Father and said the Father would give the Holy Spirit to those who ask Him. The Holy Spirit is another comforter; one in nature and union with Christ who would be our guide and teacher as He would dwell in us. Christ also admonished His followers to wait until they received this power. On the Day of Pentecost the arrival of the Holy Spirit ushered in the church age.

The word power comes from different Greek words which, in the King James Bible, were all translated to the word power. *Exousia* appears sixty-one times and has the meaning privilege, force, capacity, competence, freedom, token of control, authority, jurisdiction, liberty, power, right or strength: it is translated in newer versions as authority. *Dunamis*, (force, miraculous power, abundance, ability, might, worker of miracles, power, strength, or mighty work) is translated power seventy-one times. The power Jesus was talking about which came on the Day of Pentecost was active in the apostles and Stephen, Phillip, Phillip's daughters, and Timothy to name a few. It was not given to the apostles only but to all who receive the Baptism of the Holy Spirit. *Dunamis* is the root word for dynamite and *dyne* which is a unit of work. The power was given to have some dynamite; to have explosive power for the working of miracles, healing, salvation and being a witness for Christ.

Chapter Review

Let us review the truth in these previous passages. (1) John the Baptist foretold of one greater than himself who would baptize with the Holy Spirit and fire.

(2) When the Holy Spirit abode on Christ it signified He would baptize you with the Holy Spirit and fire.

(3) Christ said the Father would give the Holy Spirit to those who ask.

(4) Christ said if anyone would thirst and come to Him and out of His belly (innermost being, spirit) would flow rivers of living water.

(5) The Holy Spirit is to be a comforter and the Promise of the Father.

(6) The Holy Spirit endues with power.

(7) It was so vital Christ commanded His disciples to tarry in Jerusalem until they were endued with power.

(8) The Holy Spirit came with the sound of a mighty rushing wind and cloven tongues of fire which sat upon each of them.

(9) All the one hundred and twenty received the Holy Spirit and all spoke with tongues as the Spirit gave them utterance.

My experience was not exactly the same as when the Holy Spirit came on the Day of Pentecost but, it in no way, contradicts the experience the disciples had on that day or any of the following experiences recorded in the book of Acts. Whoever is thirsty and will ask the Father, the promise is that all may have a similar experience. Jesus emphasized to wait for the Holy Spirit to the disciples and those gathered in the upper room. The Day of Pentecost was when the Holy Spirit was given and they were to be ready to receive the Promise of the Father. They needed the Holy Spirit and were commanded to wait for the Holy Spirit. Should we also have a time of waiting or seeking the same Promise of the Father?

Chapter Three: The Baptism in the Holy Spirit

The importance of the baptism of the Holy Spirit and exactly what this baptism is will be the subject of this chapter. The Bible has numerous references and teaching about the Holy Spirit. There is no better guide to use when searching for truth. The experiences of the early church will serve as a guide for this chapter.

The second verse of chapter two in the book of Acts relates the sound from heaven as of a rushing mighty wind and it filled the whole house where they were sitting. The word for Spirit, in the Hebrew, is *ruwach* which is translated wind from the root of the same word which means to blow, i.e. breathe. The word in the Greek (the New Testament was written in Greek) is the word *pneuma*. It is from the root word pneo which means to breathe or a breeze. *Pneuma* is a current of air, breath or a breeze and by analogy a spirit, Christ's Spirit or the Holy Spirit. The doctrine or teaching on the Holy Spirit is pneumatology. When a mechanic uses an air driven tool he is using a pneumatic tool. The very word used in the Old Testament and in the New Testament carries the meaning of air or wind. When the sound from heaven was as a rushing mighty wind it was a physical evidence of the Holy Spirit.

The next verse brings forth another physical evidence; there appeared to them divided tongues as of fire and sat upon each of them. Moses had an experience with a bush which was burning but was not consumed by the fire. Exodus chapter three and verse two says the Angel of the Lord appeared to him in a flame of fire from the midst of a bush. When the nation of Israel left Egypt the Lord went before them by day in a pillar of cloud to lead the way and by night in a pillar of fire to give them light, so as to go by day and night. (Exodus 13:21) Mount Horeb burned as with fire and the Lord spoke out of the midst of the fire. (Deut. 4:12)

When Gideon made an offering, the Angel of the Lord extended His staff and touched the meat and unleavened bread and fire rose out of the rock and consumed the meat and unleavened bread. (Judges 6:21) When Elijah challenged the prophets of Baal the fire of the Lord fell and consumed the burnt sacrifice, and the wood, and the stones and the dust, and it licked up the water that was in the trench. (I Kings 18:38) In the first chapter of Second Kings fire twice came down and burnt up two captains and their fifty men. Elijah was separated from Elisha by the appearance of a chariot of fire with horses of fire and was then taken to heaven. (2 Kings 2:11) When Solomon had finished praying, fire came down from heaven and consumed the burnt offering and the sacrifices and the glory of the Lord filled the temple. (2Chronicles 7:1) Isaiah chapter six records a vision of the glory of the Lord and seraphim (the burning ones), Ezekiel's vision in chapter one verse four speaks of a great cloud with raging fire engulfing itself. The prophet Joel also mentions fire and pillars of smoke. (Joel 2:30)

When the Holy Spirit came with the noise of a rushing mighty wind there was no doubt it was the wind or Spirit of the Lord. The divided tongues of fire was another physical manifestation of the presence of Almighty God. We miss the significance of the tongues of fire if we do not understand how often the Lord appeared or demonstrated His power by fire. The Jewish culture understood the fire as the presence and sometimes the judgment of the Lord. The fire was also a cleansing as when the coal was touched to the lips of Isaiah. John the Baptist said Christ would baptize you with the Holy Spirit and with fire. The experience of receiving the Holy Spirit and speaking with other tongues came with the presence of wind and the anointing of fire. There was no doubt this was the presence and movement of the Lord.

They began to speak with other tongues as the Spirit gave them utterance. When the sound occurred the multitude came together. It might have sounded like a tornado but was loud enough to gather a crowd. These were people from every nation under heaven according to verse five. They heard them speak in their own language which caused an utter amazement because all the speakers were Galileans. (The people from different regions were in Jerusalem for the feast of Pentecost) The Galileans were not the elite of society. At least sixteen regions or cultures are mentioned and each heard their native tongue being spoken and telling of the wonderful works of God.

In this passage we know that tongues may be a known language to those who hear. Paul states in the book of Corinthians he spoke with the tongues of men and angels. The language may be known by someone who happens to hear or it may be totally foreign to the hearer. What is important to remember is that the language is not known by the one speaking. This is an unknown tongue, it is not known by the one speaking. Paul explains that it is the spirit in a person that prays in a tongue but the understanding is unfruitful or not understood by the one speaking. Paul stated *he would pray with the spirit and pray with the understanding and he would sing in or with the spirit and also sing with the understanding.* (I Cor. 14:14-15) When a person speaks, prays or sings with the understanding it is done with whatever language is normal for their culture. It is what they know and were taught. It is done with their understanding and intelligence. When one speaks, prays or sings with the spirit, the spirit in a person is using the physical voice to speak but it does not go through the soul and brain. There is no understanding as to what is being brought forth.

This phenomena of using your spirit to bring forth an unknown tongue is amazing and supernatural but should be normal. Many people I have talked with about this are perplexed and apprehensive. To me this is no more puzzling than the change occurring when accepting Christ as Lord and Savior and becoming His disciple. The wind and the divided tongues of fire were an assurance to the believers in the upper room. The Lord did not want any doubts about the experience. We also may rest in the peace of knowing that praying in an unknown tongue is the Lord's will and desire. It is the Lord's desire as evidenced from the array of scriptures given in these first two chapters. The scriptures are showing the promise and appearance of the Holy Spirit. Those scriptures also give an understanding of this supernatural utterance and I believe an assurance of the Lord and Father giving this gift to us.

When Peter stood and spoke to the multitude, who gathered to witness the pouring forth of the Holy Spirit and speaking with tongues, he concluded by saying; *"Repent and let every one of you be baptized in the name of Jesus Christ for the remission of sins; and you shall receive the gift of the Holy Spirit. For the promise is to you and to your children and to all who are afar off, as many as the Lord our God will call."* (Acts 2:38-39) This is a promise to all who come to Christ throughout the church age. A few verses later (Vs. 42) states this; *And they continued steadfastly in the apostles' doctrine and fellowship, in the breaking of bread, and in prayers.* What was the doctrine or teaching they continued along with fellowship, communion and praying. They taught about speaking in tongues along with the teaching on salvation, the Lord's Supper, and fellowship.

Acts chapter three relates the story of healing a lame man who had never walked. It was the power of the Holy Spirit demonstrated and resulted in five thousand believing in the Lord. In chapter four and verse thirteen the rulers, elders and scribes *saw the boldness of Peter and John and perceived they were uneducated and untrained men, they marveled and realized they had been with Jesus.* Not only had they been with Jesus they now had the power of the Holy Spirit flowing in and through them. One aspect of the Baptism of the Holy Spirit is a greater boldness and ability to expound on the things of God even to the degree it amazes others. I remember many times being asked a question and not knowing the answer I would pray and ask God for the answer because I was going to start giving an answer. I learned some amazing truth by hearing what came from me as I would answer.

And Stephen, full of faith and power (dunamis), did great wonders and signs among the people. (Acts 6:8) And they were not able to resist the wisdom and the Spirit by which he spoke. (Acts 6:10) Stephen was a deacon not an apostle. He was faithful in what he was given to do and the Lord enlarged his ministry. Philip, another deacon went to Samaria and preached and converted multitudes and they saw the miracles, the deliverances and healings.

Now when the apostles who were at Jerusalem heard that Samaria had received the word of God, they sent Peter and John to them, who, when they had come down, prayed for them that they might receive the Holy Spirit. For as yet He had fallen upon none of them. They had only been baptized in the name of the Lord Jesus. Then they laid hands on them, and they received the Holy Spirit. And when Simon saw that through the laying on of the apostles' hands the Holy Spirit was given, he offered them money, saying, "Give me this power also, that anyone on whom I lay hands may receive the Holy Spirit." (Acts 8:14-19) For some this is a controversial passage because it does not say they spoke with tongues. I believe they spoke with tongues simply because that was the normal experience and there had to be a dynamic occurrence to lead Simon to believe beyond any doubt the Holy Spirit was received by those who were prayed for by the apostles.

When Ananias received a vision to pray for Paul he prayed for Paul that he might receive his sight and be filled with the Holy Spirit. It doesn't record in this passage he spoke with tongues but he was filled with the Holy Spirit. Paul, in his writings said he spoke with tongues. (Acts 9:9-17)

Peter and Cornelius both received an instructional vision which brought Peter to the house of Cornelius. "And the following day they entered Caesarea. Now Cornelius was waiting for them and had called together his relatives and close friends...While Peter was still speaking these words, the Holy Spirit fell upon those who heard the word. And those of the circumcision who believed were astonished, as many as came with Peter, because the gift of the Holy Spirit had been poured out on the Gentiles also. For they heard them speak with tongues and magnify God. Then Peter answered, *"Can anyone forbid water, that these should not be baptized who have received the Holy Spirit just as we have?"* (Acts 10:24, 44-47)

They believed and accepted the Lord while Peter was preaching. They were baptized into the body of Christ. They received the baptism of the Holy Spirit from Christ and spoke with tongues. After this they were baptized in water. The soul is baptized into the body of Christ. The spirit is baptized into the Holy Spirit by the Lord Jesus Christ. The body is baptized into water. There is a baptism for each part of man, the soul, the body and the spirit. The Holy Spirit baptizes the soul into the body of Christ when one accepts the Lord. The spirit is baptized by Christ into the Holy Spirit and the body is baptized into water as a confession of faith. When Peter was telling the story to the apostles and brethren in Jerusalem he remembered the statement from Christ when he said, "John indeed baptized with water but you shall be baptized with the Holy Spirit." He also stated God gave them the same gift. That gift was the Holy Spirit and those with Peter heard them speak with tongues. When Peter remembered the Lord saying they would be baptized with the Holy Spirit he witnessed the truth of that not only on Pentecost, but also in Samaria and with the gentiles also at the house of Cornelius.

And it happened, while Apollos was at Corinth, that Paul, having passed through the upper regions, came to Ephesus. And finding some disciples he said to them, *"Did you receive the Holy Spirit when you believed?"* So they said to him, *"We have not so much as heard whether there is a Holy Spirit."* And he said to them, *"Into what then were you baptized?" So they said, "Into John's baptism." Then Paul said, "John indeed baptized with a baptism of repentance saying to the people that they should believe on Him who would come after him that is, on Christ Jesus." When they heard this they were baptized in the name of the Lord Jesus. And when Paul had laid hands on them the Holy Spirit came upon them, and they spoke with tongues and prophesied.* (Acts19:1-6) The chapter also reveals Paul stayed in that region and God worked unusual miracles by the hands of Paul.

The book of Acts traces the early history of the church. The church started ministering after the Holy Spirit came on the Day of Pentecost. Speaking in tongues was a part of the apostles' doctrine as evidenced by what happened on the Day of Pentecost, by what happened in Samaria, by what happened to Cornelius, by what happened to Paul and by what happened to the disciples Paul met at Ephesus twenty years after the Holy Spirit came on Pentecost.

Chapter Review

The wind and fire at Pentecost were symbolic of the presence of God. Many people when they receive the baptism of the Holy Spirit have an experience of heat in their body. The passages from the book of The Acts of the Apostles show the experiences of being baptized with or in the Holy Spirit were normal for the church.

Tongues are an unknown language to the person speaking it. It may or may not be known to the hearer. The speech comes from our spirit not the brain or soul. The accent, tone, and inflection are not common to the speaker as well. When you allow the Holy Spirit to speak through you, not only do you not recognize the language, but commonly the voice does not even sound like yours. Speaking in tongues as a result of the baptism of the Holy Spirit is not only a sign to others; it is a confirmation to the individual that The Holy Spirit must be involved because I couldn't have done this alone.

The next chapter reveals some Biblical reasons to pray in tongues and may open the eyes of your understanding to this wonderful gift.

Chapter Four: Reasons to Pray in Tongues

The practice of praying and speaking in tongues is not always understood even by those who enjoy and utilize this gift. A lack of understanding inhibits the manifestation in the lives of others who are less comfortable with the idea of tongues. One of the more frequent statements I have heard is "Why should I speak a lot of gibberish if I have no clue as to what I am saying?" Well, I prayed and said," God, if you want me to have this gift just give it to me," is another position. That the Lord wants you to have this gift is evident with the scriptures given in the first three chapters. Why are those scriptures in the Bible? Is it just to tell us it was for the early church? There are plenty of verses which explain and magnify our understanding which we will explore as we continue this study. The question remains, are we willing to seek the Lord diligently until we receive what He offers?

"My people are destroyed for lack of knowledge." (Hosea 4:6) The word destroyed according to Strong's Concordance is a root word which means to be dumb or silent; to fail or perish; to cease or be cut down; be brought to silence or be undone. The truth is when we do not understand or reject the knowledge of God or the Biblical truth we miss the blessings, grace and mercy of the Lord. If I do not understand the Lord forgives me and cleanses me when I confess my sin I would live my life with guilt and condemnation not knowing the grace and mercy of the Lord. The knowledge of that truth enriches my life. The truth of and the reasons to speak or pray in tongues is not any different. Knowledge and understanding of the purpose and benefits of tongues may remove many doubts and inhibitions concerning tongues.

A word of caution is interjected here. Christ said if you spoke against Him it would be forgiven but to blaspheme against the Holy Spirit would not be forgiven. (Mt. 12:31-32; Mk.3:28-30; Lk. 12:10). That is a very serious statement. Strong's Concordance defines the word blasphemy as to vilify, to speak impiously, defame and speak evil of. The Pharisees were attributing the Work of Christ to the power of Satan. Few people would blaspheme against the Holy Spirit knowing the consequences would be eternal. We should have a reverence for the Holy Spirit and His working in our lives. Tongues are an outworking of the Holy Spirit. To blaspheme against tongues is put yourself in a precarious position. I have had one person whom I prayed with and he received the Baptism of the Holy Spirit come to me years later and told me, "I told God I didn't want the baptism of the Holy Spirit and speaking in tongues because I don't see any value and purpose in it." Sadly, he died in his early forties. I am not saying rejecting the Holy Spirit is the reason or cause of death, but I have often wondered what the result of that rejection was.

My parents started going to an established church and met with the pastor to say they believed in the baptism of the Holy Spirit and speaking in tongues. He welcomed them but said he didn't want speaking in tongues to be a distraction in the services. It wasn't long before church members were meeting in my parent's living room and receiving the Holy Spirit as well as speaking with tongues. Later the pastor spoke from the pulpit saying the practice of speaking in tongues was getting out of hand although it never occurred in a service. He said it had to stop and anyone who practiced speaking in tongues should leave the church. People did leave. Three months later the church was no longer in existence. These are two experiences from my life. I relate them for you to ponder and realize we should reverence the Holy Spirit and be cautious with our speech concerning the Holy Spirit and His work in our lives.

With that note of caution let us proceed to understand why we should pray in tongues and what the benefit is to be in our lives. (1) *"Therefore tongues are a sign, not to those who believe but to unbelievers; but prophesying is not for unbelievers but for those who believe."* (1 Cor. 14:22) Tongues spoken in church are a sign to unbelievers. Tongues are an indication of the supernatural power of the Holy Spirit indwelling believers. On the Day of Pentecost it was a sign to the multitude who gathered in Jerusalem. They heard them speaking the wonderful works of God and three thousand were saved that day. Tongues are a sign which can lead others to want to know Christ.

(2) "But you shall receive power when the Holy Spirit has come upon you; and you shall be witnesses to Me in Jerusalem, and in all Judea and Samaria, and to the end of the earth." (Acts1:8) When you receive the Holy Spirit you are also receiving the power to be witnesses to

Christ. This power also brings availability of the spirituals into the life of a believer. (1Cor. 12. More on this later)

(3) Speaking with tongues are a fulfillment of prophecy. It also helps in your spiritual growing. Acts 2:17-21. Peter quoted from the book of Joel after the Holy Spirit came on the Day of Pentecost. I Cor. 14:21 quotes from Isaiah chapter twenty eight and verses eleven and twelve. If we start at verse ten and look more closely at the passage in Isaiah and the context we will discover a few hidden gems of truth. *"For precept must be upon precept, precept upon precept, line upon line, line upon line, here a little, there a little. For with stammering lips and another tongue He will speak to this people, to whom He said, "This is the rest with which you may cause the weary to rest," and, "this is the refreshing;" Yet they would not hear.* (Is. 28:10-12) First let us look at verse ten with precept upon precept, line upon line, here a little, there a little. What does this mean? It is the way we learn. I teach martial arts and a foundation must be laid to build upon. The basic movements give to the body the coordination to do more advanced movements. We learn the alphabet and then we use the letters to form words; the words become sentences; the sentences become paragraphs and paragraphs become stories or teaching information. The Holy Spirit starts teaching us about the ways and things of God.

"But as it is written: Eye has not seen, nor ear heard, nor have entered into the heart of man the things which God has prepared for those who love Him. (Is. 64:4, 65:17) But God has revealed them to us through His Spirit. For the Spirit searches all things, yes, the deep things of God. For what man knows the things of a man except the spirit of man which is in him? Even so no one knows the things of God except the Spirit of God. Now we have received, not the spirit of the world, but the Spirit who is from God, that we might know the things that have been freely given to us by God. These things we also speak, not in words which man's wisdom teaches but which the Holy Spirit teaches, comparing spiritual things with spiritual. But the natural man does not receive the things of the Spirit of God, for they are foolishness to him, nor can he know them because they are spiritually discerned. (1 Cor. 2:9-14)"

This is the line upon line comparing spiritual things with spiritual. After the lame man was made whole in Acts chapter three, the thirteenth verse of chapter four says; *"Now when they saw the boldness of Peter and John and perceived that they were uneducated and untrained men, they marveled. And they realized that they had been with Jesus."* I have witnessed the improvement in the lives of many others that, after receiving the Holy Spirit they grow in understanding of the things of God. I have witnessed an improved understanding in other practical areas of life also. The Holy Spirit is the Spirit of Truth and will lead us into all truth.

(4) Praying in the spirit is a rest and refreshing. Although Paul quoted a part of the passage from Isaiah twenty-eight in 1 Corinthians when we put the passage in context it shows along with other passages the Spirit of Truth guides and leads into more truth, line upon line, precept upon precept and comparing spiritual things with spiritual. Verse twelve of Isaiah twenty-eight states; *"To whom He said, 'This is the rest with which you may cause the weary to rest and this is the refreshing"*. The stammering lips and another tongue are to be a rest and refreshing for us. Praying in the Spirit or in tongues is a rest and refreshing available if we allow the living water of the Holy Spirit to flow through us.

(5) "For he who speaks in a tongue does not speak to men but to God, for no one understands him; however in the spirit he speaks mysteries." (1 Cor. 14:2) The first part is simple and straight forward: when we speak in a tongue we are speaking to God. When Christ spoke to the Samaritan woman at the well He said they that worship God must worship Him in Spirit and in truth. Paul, when starting to write about the spirituals in chapter twelve, says this in verse three; "Therefore I make known to you that no one speaking by the Spirit of God call Jesus accursed, and no one can say that Jesus is Lord except by the Holy Spirit." When we speak in a tongue we are speaking or praying to God. Our spirit is talking or praying to God without the limitations of our soul or understanding but Paul makes it clear we will not say anything against Christ while we are speaking in tongues. There is usually one language which will flow more than any other and it is your prayer language or tongue. This does not mean you will never speak in another tongue for that is a possibility. After service one Sunday I was praying over those with needs. Four members came for prayer and I spoke or prayed over them in four distinct and different languages or tongues. Why? I don't know, but I do know I

20

was speaking to God in each of those tongues. Mark quotes Jesus as saying these signs shall follow them that believe...they shall speak with new tongues. (Mk. 16:17)

The second part of verse two says; "*however, in the spirit he speaks mysteries*" The word for mysteries in the Greek is *musterion* which means a former secret now disclosed or opened. We are speaking to God and things which were unknown are now becoming known. When Jesus gave what is known as the Lord's Prayer a part of it is; "*Your will be done on earth as it is in heaven.*" The will of the Father is done in heaven before it is manifested on earth. In the book of Job, Satan was given permission in Heaven to attack Job before it was manifested on earth. Daniel prayed and an answer was sent from Heaven but was delayed and Michael had to intervene for the answer to get to Daniel. Part of speaking in a tongue and speaking mysteries is to bring about what has already occurred in the Father's plan. It is bringing the will and desire from the spiritual realm into the physical realm. Another aspect of mysteries might be the revealing of truth as in line upon line, precept upon precept and comparing spiritual things with spiritual. Sometimes when praying in tongues you might receive an answer to a problem or situation. What was not known becomes known.

(6) "*He who speaks in a tongue edifies himself, but he who prophesies edifies the church.*" (1Cor. 14:4) If you speak in a tongue you edify yourself. This is a building up or making stronger. It is the idea of an athlete training to become stronger and better at what he does. It is not selfish; it is striving to become all you were created to be. The root of the word edify comes from the concept of laying a strong foundation or a cornerstone. It is possible Paul alluded to this also. Speaking in a tongue builds a spiritual foundation for your life.

(7) "*I wish you all spoke with tongues...*" (1Cor 14:5) The apostle Paul who wrote nearly half of the New Testament said his desire, want or wish was for all to speak in tongues. It is the desire of the Father, the Lord Jesus, the Holy Spirit and the apostle Paul that all would speak in tongues. Why would Paul write that if it were not possible and available to everyone?

(8) "How is it then brethren? Whenever you come together, each of you has a psalm, has a teaching, has a tongue, has a revelation, has an interpretation. Let all things be done for edification." (1Cor. 14:26) The

21

King James Version has every one and not each one. The meaning is clear and resounding; we have a responsibility to bring something when we, the body of Christ, comes together. If we do not believe or practice praying in tongues we would never bring a tongue to a service. This tongue may be more for the edification of the church than for us as individuals. This goes beyond ourselves and is using a tongue with interpretation to bring a blessing from the loving heart of the Father to those who gather together.

(9) *"For they heard them speak with tongues and magnify God...* (Acts 10:46) Whether or not those who were with Peter at the house of Cornelius understood what was being said is unknown but they understood they were speaking with tongues and magnifying God. Tongues are a way in which we may acknowledge and magnify the greatness of Almighty God. On the Day of Pentecost they were speaking and extolling the wonderful works of God. Praying in tongues opens a new frontier to worship and magnify God.

(10) "For if I pray in a tongue, my spirit prays, but my understanding is unfruitful. What is the conclusion then? I will pray with the spirit, and I will also pray with the understanding. I will sing with the spirit and I will also sing with the understanding." (1Cor. 14:14-15) Paul said when he prays with the spirit he doesn't understand so he will pray with the spirit and in the languages he learned. He would also sing in the spirit and sing with the understanding. "And do not be drunk with wine, in which is dissipation; but be filled with the Spirit, speaking to one another is psalms and hymns and spiritual songs, singing and making melody in your heart to the Lord, giving thanks always for all things to God the Father in the name of our Lord Jesus Christ." (Ephesians 5:18-20) "Let the word of Christ dwell in you richly in all wisdom, teaching and admonishing one another in psalms and hymns and spiritual songs, singing with grace in your hearts to the Lord."(Colossians 3:16) We may build up or edify one another with the singing of psalms and hymns and spiritual songs or we may sing in the spirit to have a melody in our heart to the Lord. This is a greater blessing than my words can describe. I have sung in the Spirit a few times over people and the results were dramatic. I have heard my mom sing in the spirit and she has a nice voice but when she sings in the Spirit there is an anointing and presence which brings a peace beyond understanding.

Being obedient and singing in the Spirit may bring great blessings to those around us.

(11) "Likewise the Spirit also helps in our weakness. For we do not know what we should pray for as we ought, but the Spirit Himself makes intercession for us with groanings which cannot be uttered." (Romans 8:26) The Spirit makes intercession for us according to the will of God. The Holy Spirit is using us to intercede. Sometimes this is not understood and at times it is in a tongue. Interceding on the behalf of others is one of the usages of a tongue or prayer language. The Spirit helps us when we do not know how to or what to pray. This is more important than what might appear on the surface. Battles are won or lost because of the obedience to prayer. Often I have a name go through my mind. Usually it is not someone I know personally. When a name keeps entering my thoughts I know I have a responsibility to pray in the Spirit for whoever it is. I have no idea how to pray for someone I have never met so I rely on praying in the Spirit. At times you may receive a dream or vision of what you are praying for under the Holy Spirit's leading.

(12) *And take the helmet of salvation and the sword of the Spirit which is the word of God; praying always with all prayer and supplication in the Spirit, being watchful to the end with all perseverance and supplication for all the saints—"* (Ephesians 6:17-18) Praying in the Spirit is a weapon to fight a spiritual battle. It is an active part of the armor of God. If you do not pray in the spirit against the principalities, against powers, against the rulers of the darkness of this age and against spiritual hosts of wickedness in the heavenly places; you are allowing them to grow and gain a greater influence in your life and the lives of those around you and in your community and even your nation. Praying in the Spirit is work and it is necessary.

(13) *"But you, beloved, building yourselves up on your most holy faith, praying in the Holy Spirit, keep yourselves in the love of God, looking for the mercy of our Lord Jesus Christ unto eternal life."* (Jude 19-20) Praying in the Holy Spirit builds our faith and helps keep us in the love of God. My faith is tried and stretched and I become weak. Praying in the Spirit builds a reservoir of faith and without faith it is impossible to please God.

(14)*But if there be no interpreter, let him keep silent in the church; and let him speak to himself, and to God.* (I Cor. 14:28) Paul was admonishing if there is no one to interpret a tongue then one should not speak out and disrupt the service but to speak to himself and to God. This verse has been used to mean you shouldn't pray or speak in tongues unless there is an interpreter. That is only the first part of the verse. The last part of the verse says to speak to himself and to God. Verse thirty two states the spirits of the prophets are subject to the prophets. This applies not only to prophets but also for any of the spirituals in operation. The Holy Spirit will not violate our will or cause us to lose control in any way. WE yield ourselves to the anointing, unction, or leading of the Holy Spirit and cooperate with Him but our spirits are under our control.

(15) *Wherefore, brethren, covet to prophesy, and do not forbid to speak with tongues. Let all things be done decently and in order.* (1 Cor. 14:39-40) We will delve into prophecy later but Paul stated emphatically: "do not forbid to speak in tongues." There is no verse which states we should not speak in tongues but this verse says do not forbid the practice. Keeping order and the decency or etiquette as we cooperate with the Holy Spirit as He moves in a service is first and foremost in the apostles teaching. The beauty and majesty of the Holy Spirit's moving unites and brings a group, fellowship or local assembly closer to the Lord Jesus Christ.

Chapter Review

Praying in tongues is a fulfillment of prophecy and a sign to unbelievers. The Spirit passes power to us as believers who accept the Holy Spirit as an active part of the Armor of God which can help in our weakness and also for our lack of knowledge for prayer as to the specific plan of God. Prayer in tongues speaks in a language that connects with God. Spiritual prayer and singing brings rest and a new dimension of refreshing to ourselves, edifies ourselves and can bring blessings as well as helping to build our faith. The Trinity desires for us to speak in tongues, cautions us to not forbid the spirit, and leaves the ability to speak in tongues under our control. Praying in tongues magnifies God, allows God to speak to the church body, and also brings power into spiritual warfare. These are many varied reasons to ask the Spirit into our lives.

Chapter Five: The Trinity Gives Gifts

Understanding that each person of the Trinity gives gifts to the church helps in understanding not only the uniqueness of the gifts but their use and functioning in the body of Christ. This chapter looks at the gifts given by each member of the Trinity.

Christ said to the disciples they would receive power after the Holy Spirit came upon them and they would be witnesses. How does that power work? How does it function in our lives? Paul wrote to the church at Corinth to explain the spirituals. In chapter twelve and verse one the word gifts is italicized which means it is not in the original text but was added to help our understanding. Without the word gifts Paul is saying, "now concerning spirituals". Throughout this book I will refer to the spirituals. Remembering it is the list of nine spirituals in First Corinthians twelve to which I am referencing will avoid confusion. In that first verse Paul stated he did not want us to be ignorant. Paul wanted the church to have knowledge and understanding of this aspect of the Holy Spirit's power ministry and how these should function and flow in the body of Christ.

Before expounding upon the spirituals and the grace or charisma gifts it is important to know a few guidelines to aid in understanding their manifestation. In verse three it is emphasized that no one speaking by the Spirit of God calls Jesus accursed and no one can say Jesus is Lord except by the Holy Spirit. All the manifestations honor the Lord Jesus Christ and draw others closer to Him. When anything happens to draw attention to a person or behavior and not Christ we should be leery and cautious. It is probably one of two situations; either a person has not grown in the grace of functioning in their cooperation with the Holy Spirit and lacks teaching and understanding, or it is the enemy trying to disrupt the service and flow of the Holy Spirit.

The Holy Spirit Gives Spirituals

"There are diversities of gifts, but the same Spirit. There are differences of ministries, but the same Lord. And there are diversities of activities, but it is the same God who works all in all. But the manifestation of the Spirit is given to each one for the profit of all." (1Cor 12:4-7) There is a diversity of gifts, but the same Spirit. In this verse the word for gifts is

charisma. This is a divine enablement, endowment or miraculous faculty. It is also the word used in verse nine, in verse twenty eight and verse thirty. The spirituals which are the subject of verses seven to eleven are the Holy Spirit's charisma gifts or spirituals.

The Lord's Gifts
There are differences of ministries but the same Lord. The word Lord here is kurios meaning supreme in authority. "And He Himself gave some to be apostles, some prophets, some evangelists, and some pastors and teachers, for the equipping of the saints for the work of ministry, for the edifying of the body of Christ,... (Eph. 4:11, 12). Christ gives gifts or presents to the church; the word used here is doma. The gifts of Christ to the church are people who are anointed to minister to others for the growth of the body of Christ.

The Father's Gifts
"And there are diversities of activities but it is the same God (Theos) who works all in all." In Romans twelve we find this passage: "Having then gifts differing according to the grace that is given to us, let us use them: if prophecy let us prophesy in proportion to our faith; or ministry, let us use it in our ministering; he who teaches, in teaching; he who exhorts, in exhortation; he who gives with liberality; he who leads with diligence; he who shows mercy with cheerfulness." Helps and administration are spoken of in chapter twelve and verse twenty-eight of First Corinthians and need to be included in the overview of gifts.

Each person of the trinity bestows gifts upon or into the body of Christ. Paul uses over half the twelfth chapter in First Corinthians to compare the church and the function of the body. As the body is not just eyes or noses or hands or feet, so the spiritual body of Christ is made of different individuals with different gifts and callings so the church may function as the Lord desires. Each member with their gifts and callings are important and needs to function for the church body to be healthy. According to the statement Paul made in Romans 11:22, the gifts and callings of God are irrevocable. When God calls a person or when one receives any type of gift they are to be used throughout their lifetime here on earth. All should grow, increase their faith and seek to improve their ability to minister with what they have received. The church should be the perfect example of unity in diversity.

For this book the Spirituals, the gifts of the Holy Spirit, will be explored. It may be another volume which explores the gifts of the Son and of the Father. The understanding of the Trinity and the unique impartation of each person is introduced here to help clarify what the Holy Spirit gives.

The Spirituals

"But the manifestation of the Spirit is given to each one for the profit of all. But one and the same Spirit works all these things, distributing to each one individually as He wills." (1 Cor. 12:7, 11) All the spirituals are given by the Holy Spirit and are given at His will or choosing. The manifestation is the exhibiting, expression or bestowment which makes open to be known or seen. We cannot force or make the spirituals operate in our lives but we learn to present ourselves as open vessels through which the power of the spirituals may flow. Paul said to earnestly desire the best gifts (12:31) He also said pursue love and desire spirituals but especially that you may prophesy (14:1). He also explained that since they were zealous for spirituals let it be for the edification of the church (14:12). We should have an intense desire for the operation or manifestation of the spirituals in our lives. The commands to desire the spirituals are a key as to how and to whom the Holy Spirit will manifest His power. If we have no desire to be used, the Holy Spirit will honor our desire. However, if we desire and seek to be used, the Holy Spirit will also honor our desire.

Paul stated in verse thirty-one of chapter twelve to desire the best gifts and yet he would show a more excellent way. All the spirituals are the best gifts. However, what the Holy Spirit desires to have flow through a person today might not be what is necessary for tomorrow's needs. The best gifts are what the Holy Spirit knows is needed for a particular situation. Prophecy may be the best gift to meet a person's needs today. Tomorrow the best gifts might be gifts of healings or the working of miracles.

This means we should desire the gifts but Paul is showing the excellent way they are to function. First Corinthians thirteen is known as the love chapter. The verses four to eight are a description of the function of love. Why is that chapter where it is.? That is a question the Holy Spirit placed in my mind. When Paul wrote his epistles they were written without the chapter and verse designations. The chapter and verse divisions were added much later. Those few verses on love were written between the teaching of the Holy Spirit's gifts and how they are to function in the church. Why take the time to explain love and how important it is at this particular location in the scriptures? Paul could have written a short epistle to any of the churches on love but the Holy Spirit chose for the treatise on love to be penned by Paul in this particular location. Why?

I spent time musing over this and praying for an answer. I know love is important and especially the agape love which Paul is sharing insights on in this passage. John, in his general epistle stated this: *"Beloved, let us love one another, for love is of God, and everyone who loves is born of God and knows God. He who does not love does not know God, for God is love. In this the love of God was manifested toward us, that God has sent His only begotten Son into the world, the we might live through Him. In this is love, not that we loved God, but that He loved us and sent His Son to be the propitiation for our sins. Beloved, if God so loved us, we also ought to love one another."* (1 Jn. 4:7-11) This tender writing urges us to love and to love one another in light of God's love for us in sending His Son to be the atonement for our sins. Paul was writing to also urge us to love in the context of the spirituals. Love should be the guiding factor for the manifestations of the Holy Spirit.

The power of the spirituals should be a manifestation of God's love into the lives of others. When we do not desire and have a passion for the love of God to flow into someone's life through these spirituals we are not allowing God's love to touch them in this manner. To me, that is both an exciting and sobering thought. It is exciting to know the love of the Father will flow into someone's life because I desire the spirituals and allow myself to be a willing vessel for their operation. It is sobering to think if I do not desire to be used others may not experience the love of God in this manner in their lives.

When Jesus healed the lepers, the blind men or the man with a withered hand was it done just to show His power? When He would cast out demons was it to show His authority? When He spoke to the Samaritan woman and told her what was happening in her life and she became an evangelist to her city was it done to show He knows our lives and thoughts? Of course Jesus did show His power and authority and the insight He was given from the Father. We should also conclude it was a manifestation of God's love flowing through the Holy Spirit abiding on Christ to touch those lives and bring them to believe in the Lord.

But earnestly desire the best gifts and I will show you that they are an expression of the never failing love of God reaching into someone's life. Pursue love and desire spiritual gifts but especially that you may continue prophesying so the people will know how much I love them. Even so you, since you are zealous for spiritual gifts let it be for the edification or building of the church that you seek to excel so my people will know the great love I have for them. I have taken the concept of the spirituals being a manifestation of the love of God and placed the 'love' concept in those verses. Does it change your viewpoint of the spirituals and why they are important?

To desire the spirituals and to be used by the Holy Spirit is not to draw attention to ourselves. It is not to promote what we do. It is to have passion and compassion to see the love of God poured into people's lives so they will accept the love gift of God's Son and have their lives forever changed to become followers of Christ. It is impossible to think of the ministry of Christ without acknowledging the miracles He performed. Christ said the works that I do you shall do also and greater works because He was going to the Father and would send the Holy Spirit to indwell in us. How many would believe that Jesus of Nazareth was truly the Son of God if He didn't do any of the miraculous accounts we know about. I do not want to impinge upon any aspect of the ministry of Christ but earnestly pray that we desire the spirituals and desire to be a sensitive, tender vessel to allow the manifestation of God's love to flow through us to touch those in our world. I will explore the verses in Chapter thirteen in a later chapter.

The purpose for writing this book is not so the world has another book on the Holy Spirit and the gifts. It is to open our understanding by presenting a different viewpoint or way of seeing the spirituals. The concept of loving those in need by being sensitive to the moving of the Holy Spirit and becoming that willing vessel is my heart's desire for you. To be willing to learn about the grace and flow of the Holy Spirit through the spiritual gifts and to move with the anointing is my desire for those reading these words. What if my lack of desire was a factor in the continuing suffering of others when God wants to love and touch their lives in some miraculous way? What if my lack of desire to prophesy and build others allows them to remain depressed and living below the high calling of the Lord? How many lives will remain under the power of a demonic stronghold because I do not desire the spirituals? To think these thoughts causes me to renew my desire to be more sensitive and willing to be used. Whoever crosses paths with you this day, week or month may be a person the Father desires to pour His love into. Are we going to be that willing servant whom the Lord uses to love them? Please pray for the desire to be used in the spirituals and answer yes to the question of being a willing servant.

Chapter Review

The Holy Spirit gives the spirituals listed in First Corinthians and chapter twelve. These will be expounded in the next chapters. These Divine enablements are available to us; we are to desire and seek after the best gifts and especially to continue prophesying. Christ gives the gift of people with a special calling on their lives to the church to help the church grow. See Ephesians chapter four starting with verse eleven for a greater understanding of why the gifts Christ gives are important. Romans twelve list the Charis or grace gifts of the Father. The spirituals or gifts of the Holy Spirit are a manifestation of God's love and should flow with His grace and love. We must be willing to be used and continually desire for the spirituals to be manifested in our lives.

Chapter Six: Vocal Gifts

The next chapters are devoted to an understanding of the nine spirituals listed in First Corinthians twelve. The gifts are commonly divided into three categories. (1) Vocal gifts: different kinds of tongues, the interpretation of tongues and prophecy. (2) Revelation gifts: the word of knowledge, the word of wisdom and discerning of spirits. (3) Power gifts: the working of miracles, the gift of faith and gifts of healings. This chapter introduces the vocal gifts and the following chapters explore the other gifts in more detail.

"..to another the working of miracles, to another prophecy, to another discerning of spirits, to another different kinds of tongues, to another the interpretation of tongues." (1 Cor. 12:10) *"Pursue love, and desire spiritual gifts, but especially that you may prophesy. For he who speaks in a tongue does not speak to men but to God, for no one understands him; however in the spirit he speaks mysteries. But he who prophesies speaks edification and exhortation and comfort to men. He who speaks in a tongue edifies himself, but he who prophesies edifies the church. I wish you all spoke with tongues, but even more that you prophesied; for he who prophesies is greater than he who speaks with tongues, unless he interprets, that the church may receive edification."* (1 Cor. 14:1-5)

Tongues are a personal expression of prayer, intercession and praise to God. When guided by or anointed by the Holy Spirit the vocalization of a tongue and the interpretation thereof is equal to a prophecy given in the known language of the assembled believers. Paul also wrote in verse twenty seven and twenty eight: *"If anyone speaks in a tongue let there be two or at the most three, each in turn and let one interpret. But if there is no interpreter, let him keep silent in church, and let him speak to himself and to God."* To have every one speak in their personal tongue and have no interpretation becomes a disruption in the service. Paul admonishes to let everything be done decently and in order. The whole order of service is to build or edify the believer and to honor and worship the Lord. Paul's admonition is not against the practice and use of tongues, interpretation and prophecy but only that it is within the flow and grace of a service.

"How is it then brethren? Whenever you come together, each of you has a psalm, has a teaching, has a tongue, has a revelation, has an interpretation. Let all things be done for edification." (1 Cor. 14:26) Not only are all things to be done for edification but each one should bring something to the meeting. The King James translated each one to 'every one'. The meaning is clear: each and every one should bring something to the assembly. The church was not meant to be a spectator experience, where you go to sit quietly and observe what is going on. It is to be a dynamic interaction from all the believers to each other and to the Lord. I am sad to see the church of the living God become more like a sporting event where people go and watch light shows and presentations for their spiritual entertainment. What I see in Paul's teaching is a more personal involvement.

"Therefore tongues are for a sign, not to those who believe but to unbelievers: but prophesying is not for unbelievers but for those who believe. Therefore if the whole church comes together in one place, and all speak with tongues, and there come in those who are uninformed or unbelievers, will they not say that you are out of your mind? But if all prophesy, and an unbeliever or an uninformed person comes in, he is convinced by all, he is convicted by all. And thus the secrets of his heart are revealed; and so falling down on his face, he will worship God and report that God is truly among you." (1 Cor. 14:22-25) The first part of this passage is referring to the quote from Isaiah in the verses preceding these verses. Tongues may be a sign of the presence of the Lord to unbelievers as tongues were a sign on the Day of Pentecost. I remember hearing tongues before I accepted the Lord and I sensed the spiritual power and was fearful in the presence of the Lord.

If all prophesy and reveal the secrets of someone's heart they will worship God and report God is truly among you. I had a friend come to the service one morning and in our church we prophesy and speak edification, exhortation and comfort to those attending the service especially those who are present for the first time. This scripture was real and living in his life that day. That should be normal.

"..especially that you may prophesy"

"..But he who prophesies speaks edification and exhortation and comfort to men."

"..but he who prophesies edifies the church.:

:..but even more that you prophesied; for he who prophesies is greater than he who speaks with tongues, unless he interprets that the church may receive edification."

"..by prophesying..."

"But if all prophesy..."

"For you can all prophesy one by one, that all may learn and all may be encouraged."

"Therefore, brethren, desire earnestly to prophesy, and do not forbid to speak with tongues."

Eight times Paul spoke of prophecy or prophesying in the fourteenth chapter of First Corinthians. He said to desire spirituals but especially prophecy and again to desire earnestly to prophesy. Why is it that so little of this is happening in the body of Christ? It is to build up the church when assembled and to build up individuals when it is done one on one. Is there any who does not need building up or made stronger? This is the treatise of "Let the Living Waters Flow" which I authored and was published in 2014. Prophecy is arising from the dust of neglect and being used according to the Biblical guidelines to once again be a tool to strengthen and build the body of Christ.

Paul wrote that we could all prophesy one by one that all may learn and all may be encouraged. All means all and no one is excluded. Prophecy is to edify, exhort and comfort. I want to encourage every reader to make an effort to edify, exhort and comfort. If you are willing to be used the scripture says all can prophesy. You are a part of the all. One fear or concern I have heard from others is they do not know what to say or are afraid of saying something wrong. When you speak out in a service and it is just your desire and not the Holy Spirit's it may just be an exhortation to the body. The Holy Spirit will use willing vessels and not those who refuse to yield and speak out. If you are speaking to someone within the guidelines to edify, exhort and comfort you will never be wrong. It might just be you speaking because we all miss what the Holy Spirit wants at times, but you are going to be speaking goods things to someone. When we are in harmony with the Holy Spirit the words may have a greater impact and may even be life changing for the hearer. Prophecy will occur when we are obedient and yielded to the Holy Spirit.

Tongues and their interpretation equals prophesy. To prophesy is to speak to men to edify, exhort and comfort. Remember we are in the arena of manifesting the spirituals given and directed by the Holy Spirit. When the Holy Spirit is using a person in this manner they are bringing to the assembly a message to build, encourage or comfort from the Heavenly throne room. It becomes a supernatural message from the loving throne of the Father brought into the physical realm by cooperation with and yielding to the Holy Spirit.

To make this clear an example from the physical may help in spiritual understanding. If I went to visit my dad, sat and spoke about him and expressed my love for him and never gave him the opportunity to say a word you might think that is strange and a little weird. If I did that once a week for years you might think there was something seriously wrong with me. Why would I never give my dad a chance to talk when we met together? That is far from the normal aspects of a relationship. Would I be content in that relationship? Would my dad be content in that relationship? If those questions made you stop and think then so should the next question. Why do we do this to our Heavenly Father when we gather at 'church'? Do you think He is satisfied with that expression of our relationship with Him?

Think about tongues along with the interpretation or prophecy being a loving communication from our Heavenly Father. Would your earthly father want to talk with you when you came for a visit? I believe our Heavenly Father desires to speak with us thousands of times more than our earthly parent desires to talk when we visit. What are we going to do to allow our Father to speak to us? Yield to the leading of the Holy Spirit and be that willing vessel. I do not want to miss what my Father has to say and I desire an intimate relationship with Him. I believe the Father absolutely desires to communicate with His children through the spirituals every time the church comes together.

The way spirituals are manifested is by cooperation with and yielding to the Holy Spirit. You may feel a gentle leading. You may sense an urge to speak. You may become nervous and feel as though you are on fire. How you are personally led by the Holy Spirit may be unique to you. You may feel a stirring or bubbling from within you which continues until you speak forth. You may see the color green and to you it means to go with a prophecy. Our walk with the Lord is by learning, yielding and being sensitive to Him. It is the same with the manifestation of the spirituals. It is yielding to the Holy Spirit. There is not a handbook to reveal how the Holy Spirit will move in and through you. But rest assured all can prophesy; that is a promise from God.

Paul wrote to Timothy and spoke of the gifts he received through prophecy. Paul also wrote about a woman prophesying with her head uncovered. In First Thessalonians he wrote to not despise or think lightly of prophecy. These are a few instances where prophecy is mentioned in the Bible. There are others. It should be a normal part of our lives. We should also honor prophecy and the prophecies which we receive. I have been given prophecies which I have written: I gain encouragement by reading and praying over them.

As we traverse the ocean of spiritual gifts and how they are to be used we must remember all the manifestations are from God through the Holy Spirit and flow from the throne room of love. Keeping this in mind will eliminate prophecies which are judgmental, which have personal directives or are from a person who just erred in the delivery. If it does not edify, exhort and comfort pray about it and decide if you should keep it and allow the prophecy to influence your life or discard it. All should be done in love, grace and mercy with tenderness and compassion.

As there is not a handbook on exactly how the manifestations occur and what you will feel or know when the Holy Spirit desires to use you, how do you function with or flow in the grace of the spirituals? Read and study and ask the Holy Spirit to guide and teach you. He came to be a helper and to teach and lead us into all truth. Sometimes a large ocean liner will drop anchor away from shore where the water is deep so the ship is not grounded by shallow water. Smaller boats may be used to transport cargo or people to the dock. Imagine the Holy Spirit is a large ship and tongues and prophecy are the smaller boats to transport the other gifts or spirituals to the dock of someone's life. Praying in the spirit or a tongue will help your sensitivity to the leading and outflow of other gifts. Prophecy may bring forth a word of knowledge or word of wisdom as you are speaking. By being sensitive and yielding to the Holy Spirit, which is what happens when we pray or prophesy, the other spirituals ride on that boat of prayer and or prophecy.

I was speaking to a man in church a word of encouragement through prophecy when I started telling him about some underhanded activities at his job. I also stated that if he continued doing his job to the best of his ability and did not say a word in his defense God would intervene and everything would work out. What started as a prophecy brought a word of knowledge and a word of wisdom. Three weeks later he stood in church and said his supervisor had a friend who was working under him and he wanted to place his friend in his (the man in our church) position. The supervisor was writing false reports and trying to discredit the man from our church. The owner of the company discovered what the supervisor was doing and fired the supervisor and the friend he was trying to promote. The owner then promoted the man from our church to the position his supervisor had. He said it was hard not to defend himself, but he heeded the words spoken to him and God worked everything for his benefit. I did not know nor was it revealed to me exactly what was occurring at his job. I felt and spoke what I believed came from the Holy Spirit. I am not saying the other spirituals work only by or through prophecy or after praying in the spirit. It is a way they have manifested in my life and I write this only as one example of the Holy Spirit's leading.

Paul took time to explain the spirituals in three chapters of First Corinthians. Obviously the church at Corinth needed the teaching but in the wisdom of the Holy Spirit it was also written for our learning and understanding. Little more than a casual mention of the other spirituals is noted with the emphasis being on tongues, the interpretation of a tongue and prophecy along with admonitions to be decent and orderly and seek to edify the church. The argument could be made that the church at Corinth was misusing the gifts and that is true. That does not negate the fact these chapters are a part of the Bible and are to guide our use of the spirituals also. I believe there is an importance to these chapters which has either been ignored or thrown out of the churches today. Our Father desires to speak to us. The Holy Spirit is waiting for us to desire His manifestation so the love of the Father and our Lord Jesus Christ may flow and bless the church.

Chapter Review

Tongues are for our use privately and also to build the church when it is interpreted (not translated) in a service. The meaning comes through without it being an exact translation. Tongues may be a sign to unbelievers and prophecy may reveal someone's heart or the treasure inside a person. Prophecy is to edify, exhort and comfort and may be used individually or corporately. Prophecy is possible for every person if they desire to be used. The heavenly Father wants to communicate with His children. All gifts are a manifestation of the Love of God.

Chapter Seven: Ministry of Tongues

The next four chapters are an in-depth look at the vocal gifts. I pray these chapters open the eyes of your understanding to see the beauty of these gifts. Their function and usage is very important to the growth of the body of Christ and should have a place of preeminence in our services. They are not to be above worship or the Word of God as all should be in balance.

The vocal gifts: tongues, interpretation, and prophecy, seem so different. However, when they are applied together by the Holy Spirit, the interpretation of a tongue equals prophecy. Now in this chapter I want to share about the ministry of tongues. This includes the ways praying in tongues benefits and helps us as well as the many different kinds of tongues: tongues for different purposes and tongues of different languages. This is personal ministry but some applications could resound in corporate settings in a church service or a gathering of believers.

Tongues are a language the soul has never learned; it is imparted to our spirit by the Holy Spirit. Our personal prayer language flows from our spirit, a gift given to us by the Holy Spirit for our use in communicating with and praising God. When we open ourselves to be used by the Holy Spirit to bring forth a tongue to others the flow is different. While we still have control over our vocalization of sound, the language, accent, intensity, and actual message is provided by the Holy Spirit. So we can wait to bring forth the message or refuse altogether, however, the way we bring it forth is under the control of the Holy Spirit. It has a different feel than praying in our prayer tongue. While to first timers it may be a bit scary, giving a tongue is interesting and exciting.

Tongues are to edify ourselves. Praying in tongues may help an individual overcome the wounds of daily living. They are a spiritual source to build your stamina and your fortitude as well as for your healing. Our stamina is needed to endure a test or a trial. Our fortitude gives us that never give up, never give in to the enemy and to have faith in the word of God as our hope for the journey. It is all part of edifying oneself for the journey of life. There is a power in speaking or praying in tongues. Praying from your spirit allows your prayers to affect the spirit world in ways we may only imagine. Speaking forth in the spirit brings spiritual life to your environment. Few things change the world around us as powerfully and dynamically as praying in the spirit.

The root of the word edifies means a dwelling or structure. It is an architectural term from laying the foundation to having a complete dwelling. It is also to make stronger or better. Praying in the spirit may be building the foundation and for the upkeep in your life and ministry. That is a powerful tool for becoming who we were created to be. Prayer to God can result in a spiritual protection around families and open hearts to receive blessing, guidance and grace. Praying in the Spirit is a more powerful way to communicate these needs to God with the guidance of the Holy Spirit. That is not to imply there will not be troubles and trials, but tongues are a spiritual force that influences not only the hearts but also the circumstances.

Praying in the spirit is a builder of faith. Jude twenty states; "But you, beloved, building yourselves up in your most holy faith, praying in the Holy Spirit". This word, building, is a combination of edifying and from a place of or to raise up as to build. But here it is not referring to yourself, but to your faith. Praying in tongues raises your faith. How exactly that works is a mystery but it does what the Bible says it will.

Praying in the spirit also can help us to build our endurance and dedication when praying for others, especially Christians I have never met. Ephesians 6:18 states, *"Praying always with all prayer and supplication in the Spirit, being watchful to this end with all perseverance and supplication for all the saints—".* This scripture concerns intercessory praying in tongues or in the Spirit. In Eph 6:18, Paul wrote we are to persevere. We are to continue our vigilance in prayer and supplication. How will I know what and how to pray for Christians I have never met? One way was is to spend time praying in the Spirit.

When Paul wrote about speaking mysteries or taking what is known in the Spirit realm and bringing that revelation into the physical or earthly realm he is talking about part of the outworking of the variety of tongues. The different kinds of tongues as a spiritual manifestation take on many forms or expressions. This is usually in contrast to prayers in our normal tongue language which edifies ourselves. The desire or need to pray in the spirit will vary with the purpose or kind of tongue given. When I pray in the spirit for myself I desire to converse with God and begin of my own desire. When praying in tongues for different reasons I will be encouraged by the Holy Spirit. I may hear a message being repeated in my spirit, or feel a bubbling to speak when being urged to give a tongue. Intercession in tongues may start as a burden or heaviness in our spirit which is released after praying in tongues. I have names come to my mind at different times. Sometimes they are a name I recognize as an athlete or someone with media presence other times they are so strange I hear them in my mind or spirit but could not pronounce what I am hearing. When it first happened I thought it was strange that weird names could come to mind. When they kept repeating themselves in my mind the Holy Spirit would nudge me to pray. After praying in tongues I usually cannot remember the names. I know for whatever reason the Holy Spirit brought them into my mind to intercede for them.

There are times when emotions are used to bring us to pray. I have felt a sadness and felt the Holy Spirit urging prayer from me. Almost any emotion may be used by the Holy Spirit to bring us to intercessory praying. My first reaction is to wonder why I am feeling what I feel. There was no change in my life or what was occurring to bring such a change in emotions. When I seek the Lord for answers I am led to pray. Praying in the Spirit brings a release of the emotions and I return to normal. We walk by faith and not by sight and the just shall live by faith. Praying in tongues is one part of living by faith and not by sight. The whole Christian experience is a blending of the supernatural and natural. It is not strange or weird or frightening. It is incredible and fascinating to allow the Holy Spirit to lead and guide through experiences which increases our love for the Lord and at the same time humbles us to realize we are allowing the variety of tongues to flow from us to manifest the love of the Father to and into a situation unknown by any natural insight or intelligence.

The different kinds of tongues are for ministry purposes. The various kinds of tongues are for much more than our personal needs. They are to minister to the body of Christ as well as magnify God. As there are many types of difficulties we face in the world several kinds of tongues are necessary to equip us for daily life from warfare to worship.

Praying in tongues is for spiritual battles

Battles are won or lost by our sensitivity to the urging of the Holy Spirit to pray in the Spirit. That is a sobering revelation. How might our lives and the world system be affected by increasing our awareness of the need to pray in tongues? The variety or different kinds of tongues is a weapon of warfare in the intercessory battlefield of the spirit world. The New Testament teaches us we are to pray. We are to pray for those in authority in the world system. We are to pray for those who watch over us. We are to continue to persevere in prayer and supplication for all saints. There are those like Anna who served in the temple with prayer and fasting which serves as an example for us. The verse in Second Chronicles says that if we humble ourselves and pray, God will hear from heaven and heal our land. If praying were a test which we had to take much of the church would get an F-. We have lost our compassion and our understanding that prayer is the foundation and catalyst for change in the world, in our lives and in the spirit realm. Lord, create in me the desire to pray in the Spirit and be humbly obedient to the task at hand.

Tongues may be for intercession

Another way the *"different kinds of tongues"* will function is through individual intercession for someone. My prayer in tongues for a person will vary and at times be totally different from what I usually pray. One service saw four individuals come for prayer. I was praying in the Spirit for each of them and spoke in four distinct and separate languages. Why? I don't know, but I do know it happened that way. I could surmise it was a way the Holy Spirit was revealing that each one was unique and special to Him.

I am not alone in these experiences. I read of a woman who was awakened with a sense to pray and saw a vision of natives surrounding a school and she interceded in the Spirit. They never attacked. Later she met one of the persons she saw in her vision. The ladies compared the time and found it to be the same date and time when the missionaries were warned they would be attacked. Everyone gathered at the school and spent the night praying. Later one of the natives came to Jesus and asked the missionary lady who were those giant men with swords who protected the school when they tried to attack.

Tongues for proclaiming and declaration

There are times when I begin to pray in the Spirit and the utterance seems to have a supernatural boldness. It becomes stronger, vibrant, and full of spiritual life with the presence of the Lord magnified. I am aware of what the change is in my speaking but it is not being directed from my mind or thoughts. I am yielded to the Holy Spirit. I am striving to list and give examples from my personal experiences to broaden the understanding of the "various kinds of tongues". I believe that the boldness carries a proclamative authority bringing a resolution from the word of God and the throne of God to meet the needs of the saints gathered together.

I was in my office and felt an urging to go to the mats and make a declaration. I thought that was interesting. I pondered on what I was to declare and why I was being led in this fashion. Again, a voice inside urged me to go the mat and make a declaration. I said, "Lord, I am not trying to be disobedient but I am not sure what this means will you help me." Those were my thoughts when again I sensed a voice with more intensity to go the mat and make a declaration. The office I use is in the same building with my martial arts school and the mat is the workout area. I walked out to the mat and looked around wondering what I was to do. I thought I have no idea what I am supposed to do so I will pray in the Spirit and see if I receive any more leading.

I voiced only a few words in tongues when the utterance became powerful and authoritative. I have heard the Lord speak in an audible voice and in my experience there is an authority to the Lord's voice that is beyond our comprehension. He is authority and that sense of authority is real and palpable when I hear Him speak. The tongue which was emanating from my being that day was the second most powerful, authoritative utterance I have heard in my life. It was unnerving. I was shaking. I heard a voice beside me whisper. "Enough is enough". My first thought was; oh holy crap, my life is never going to be the same. I apologize if the revelation of my thought at that time is not very spiritual. I was surprised by it myself but it is the thought which flashed through my mind.

I shared that illustration to bring into light another way the "different kinds of tongues" as a spiritual manifestation may occur. I was led to make a declaration. I believe it was a prophetic declaration to bring about some necessary changes in my life. More importantly it was the declaration which actually set in motion events and circumstances to bring alignment to the will and plan of God. That type or types of declarations are rare. Yes, there have been other times when I felt or sensed I was making a declaration but none compare to the magnitude of going to the mat. My experience with being led to go to the mat and make a declaration was so apprehensively awesome yet at the same time I felt the fear of the Lord permeate my being. To be inclined to start making declarations and feel the fear of the Lord is not something I am willing to arbitrarily do on my own. I am not saying I will not make a declaration but I am only going to do so when it is the will of the Holy Spirit. There is a power and authority which is delegated to and for us by the work of Christ and the leading of the Holy Spirit in which we are to be wise in the manifestation of such regardless of how it comes into our lives.

Tongues for rebuking the enemy

Tongues may bring a spiritual rebuke or a commanding of the enemy's spiritual forces to leave our presence. A friend told a story of being in prayer meetings and another man would start praying in a different language and start shaking his finger as though he was pointing at someone. After a few times he decided to go to him and tell him to knock off what he was doing. When he stood up he could not move forward and heard a voice telling him to not interfere because he was rebuking the enemy.

I recall the tone my dad would use when he was correcting something in my life. That same tone and at times the emotion of correction or rebuke is present when rebuking in tongues. This is an inner awareness of the purpose of this particular tongue.

Tongues to magnify and praise

Praise and worship is another variety of *different kinds of tongues*. Paul said he would pray in the spirit and pray with the understanding. He would also sing in the spirit and sing with the understanding. We pray, worship and praise in our normal tongue but there are occasions when someone will sing in the Spirit under the anointing which ushers in a peace and presence of the Lord which ministers and draws all who hear closer to the Lord. It is a beautiful expression of love not only to but from the Lord.

Tongues to renew and strengthen
One Sunday I was at a very low point in my life. I felt I didn't have the strength or ability to minister and preach that day. My worship leader started playing what I will describe as funky Spanish flamingo dance type music. I thought that is strange. A lady in the service started singing in the Spirit in perfect harmony to the music being played. It continued for several minutes. When the music and singing stopped I was renewed and strengthened. It served its purpose and I received a supernatural impartation. On other occasions I have heard someone pray or speak in tongues and knew in my spirit it was imparting life to my being.

Tongues open windows for other spirituals
Praying in tongues may also be the springboard for other spirituals to be manifested. Another aspect of *"different kinds of tongues"*, is praying in the Spirit and receiving dreams and visions or having another spiritual come along side to aide in some way. This may occur by praying in your normal tongue but it also is a different kind of tongue which seems to unleash spiritual understanding or insight in some way.

I have read of someone speaking in a tongue which was unknown to them but the hearers understood what was being spoken. They were sharing the glory and good news of Christ Jesus to someone who had not heard the gospel. These are a few examples of *"different kinds of tongues"*. There are many more. Tongues and the interpretation of tongues is a New Testament and church phenomenon. It is an area where the enemy does not want us to practice and use the supernatural power which is available and is manifested each and every time a believer speaks or prays in a tongue. That is too bad and so sad for the enemy of righteousness.

Tongues as a message for the church
The *"different kinds of tongues"* are not just the personal languages but goes beyond that to minister, intercede or receive revelation in some way. Another aspect is the vocal utterance in a church. This may be done in your usual language or it may be a different kind of tongue. The anointing or leading of the Holy Spirit may change a normal tongue language into another to serve His purpose. This is a vital point

to remember. You and I cannot make the change from our normal prayer language, only the Holy Spirit can bring about the various kinds of tongues and their varied aspects of ministry.

I pray this chapter enlightens you, charges your spiritual batteries, increases your understanding of this spiritual, and creates a desire to seek, desire and be zealous for not only this spiritual but for all of the spirituals.

Chapter Review

The different kinds of tongues are expressed many different ways. They are used as ministry tools to further the work of the Holy Spirit. Tongues are used to build people up. They can also renew and strengthen us. They are used to pray for others when we may not know what the real issues are to pray for. They are used to fight battles with spiritual enemies or rebuke those enemies. They are a way to praise God and may be sung. A tongue may also deliver a message to the congregation.

Chapter Eight: The Interpretation of Tongues

The interpretation of tongues is not a translation but a way of conveying the meaning of tongues. This is usually taught as tongues and the interpretation of tongues as equal to prophesy when it occurs in a church or fellowship meeting. That is what I was taught for the interpretation of tongues. I believe that is one avenue of the interpretation of tongues but I do not believe it is the only way this gift may be used or expressed.

Each of the different kinds of tongues may be interpreted when the Holy Spirit allows or brings the interpretation. When a person is praying over another person in the spirit another person may be able to interpret what is being prayed. Sometimes this is revealed to bring understanding into a person's life which was not known before. I have experienced interpretations when someone was praying for me in tongues. When The Holy Spirit allows or brings that grace into a situation it is dynamic and faith building. It is also humbling and reverential knowing and feeling the love of God being manifested.

When tongues are used to war against the enemy an interpretation may give insight into what and why the war is raging. When tongues are used for intercession the interpretation may reveal what is being prayed. Interpretation may come when any of the variety of tongues is manifested. It is the interpretation of tongues. It is not just a tongue but tongues which includes the whole sphere of the variety of tongues.

Chapter Review

Interpretation of a tongue is to bring forth its meaning to others congregated. Tongues can also be interpreted by the giver or receiver of prayer to help in understanding. I believe it is possible that interpretation to gain an understanding in any type of tongues being spoken can occur.

Chapter Nine: All May Prophesy

"For you can all prophesy one by one, that all may learn and all may be encouraged. And the spirits of the prophets are subject to the prophets." (1 Cor. 14:31, 32) You can or may all prophesy one by one. Why? So that all may learn and all may be encouraged. I would like to point out a couple items in this verse. First, all can prophesy. Who can prophesy? All, and you are one of the all mentioned here. Why? So all may learn and be encouraged. If you do not believe you may prophesy you might not ever be willing to try. It is to be done so all may learn. I believe it is so each person will learn how to yield to the Holy Spirit and with guidance in a structured setting, correction may be made. I believe prophecy is encouraging to those being spoken to and also to the one prophesying. I believe in prophesy and believe the body of Christ will learn to prophesy. Here is a paragraph from "Let the Living Waters Flow".

"It is important to prophesy. It is vital to have a passion for prophecy. It is the life-changing, spiritual healing weapon of the body of Christ which is rising from the dust of being forgotten, coming out of the closet of misunderstanding and bringing the glory of the throne room of God to be a river of living water to enlighten, bless and encourage the church of the living God. For too long prophecy has been ignored, forgotten and relegated to the back room of insignificance. We, the individuals, who are the body of Christ, will use prophecy to bring light into darkness and to move with the Holy Spirit in a river of living water. It is a key to wounded warrior healing and so much more." (Let The Living Waters Flow; 2014 Jan Coverstone, page 118)

Prophecy is to edify, comfort and exhort. With so many wounded people on the planet, prophecy is needed now more than ever. Who is not lightened or their burdens lifted by an encouraging comment. Prophecy is one of the nine spirituals or gifts of the Holy Spirit. It is also listed among the grace or Charis gifts mentioned in Romans chapter twelve. I believe prophecy may be two separate gifts or have two manifestations. One is a spiritual under the power and anointing of the Holy Spirit to speak forth a message from the throne room of the Father. I also believe it is a grace gift where one grows in ministry to edify, exhort and encourage others. Both are needed. One may be used more in private settings and the spiritual may be used more in corporate or church service settings. That is not to say that the spiritual cannot function one on one. It may be used by an individual to speak to another with the full anointing and power of the Holy Spirit.

It is interesting to note in Romans 12:8 Paul also lists exhorting as a grace gift. This is the same word used in First Corinthians when explaining that prophecy is to edify, exhort and comfort. The Greek word is *parakaleo* to exhort, to call near, invite by imploring and also comfort. The Greek word is *paraklesis* for exhortation, an imploration, solace, comfort, consolation, or entreaty. When Jesus spoke of the Holy Spirit being a comforter the word is *parakletos* a counselor or comforter. Is it possible that prophecy is close and dear to the Holy Spirit because He is the comforter who comes along our side to be with us? When prophecy draws you nearer to the Lord and comforts your being, it is a fulfilling of the ministry of the Holy Spirit as the comforter. There are thirty references in the New Testament of some form of the word exhort. We should have our words be those which comfort and draw others to Christ whether through prophecy or having our speech seasoned with grace and salt.

Does that make exhortation a form of prophecy? Are there different levels or manifestation of prophecy? Prophecy is to speak by divine intervention or influence to bring forth the mind of the Lord into a situation. Is prophecy which carries a Word of Knowledge or a Word of Wisdom different from a prophecy which does not carry any other gift with the speaking forth? Exhortation, encouragement and speaking to edify may or may not be prophecy. If the Holy Spirit's guidance is upon the words it is prophecy. What are we to do and how are we to judge? With grace and wisdom, experience and leaning on the Holy Spirit. If you are with someone who brings forth a word and they are speaking from their own heart and it edifies, comforts, or exhorts it is not wrong. It may not be prophecy but it will be encouraging and that is good.

If prophecy is a spiritual and also a grace gift then the avenues and manifestation of prophecy are much larger. The last part of the sentence in Revelation 19:10 is written this way: "*For the testimony of Jesus is the spirit of prophecy.*" The Word of God or the Bible has many prophecies and Jesus is the Word made flesh. When we share Jesus or the Bible the spirit of prophecy is present. This seems to indicate a variety of levels or manifestations of prophecy. Prophecy may not be easy to define and categorize but it should always draw us closer to the Lord and His Word.

I am presenting a few ideas and thoughts about prophecy. You do not have to agree with all of them but from what the Bible reveals about prophecy they are worthy of consideration.

When sharing from the Bible with the Holy Spirit's anointing the words are not just the logos or written word they become rhema or life giving words. This would be a prophetic declaration. The Word of God is being spoken or declared. It is being spoken and will never come back void but will accomplish what the Lord desires.

When I read the Bible and claim the promises written therein it is a form of prophetic proclamation. I am pro-claiming the promises as my own. We should all claim the promises of Jesus through the written Word as our own. I am using these two terms, although they may have similar meanings, to differentiate between what is spoken or declared to others and those which I speak or proclaim to myself. Both of these are based upon the testimony of Jesus being the spirit of prophecy.

Prophecy as a spiritual is to bring forth words from the heart of the Lord into a person or a gathering of people. They are to edify, exhort and comfort.

When a prophecy carries another spiritual with it such as a Word of Wisdom showing the direction or action to be taken it may be considered a compound prophecy. What I mean is that it has more than one element or consideration to it. This may be the form of warning to a person or nation. It may be directive for a person, congregation or nation. It is prophecy plus another spiritual.

Prophecy as a grace gift may be edifying, exhorting or comforting and may be a blend of the Word of God and also from an individual's heart or mind. These may be rhema words to bring life to an individual or group. When taking the Sword of the Spirit which is the Word (rhema) of God it is a tool of warfare. What is spoken as rhema carries life, authority and power.

Exhortation is listed as a grace gift and may also be prophetic. Prophecy is a tool to be used to change the culture, atmosphere and spiritual climate in the territory in which we live. We must strive to bring this tool into our lives and into the body of Christ. Again remember Paul's admonition to desire spirituals but especially that you may prophesy and therefore brethren desire earnestly to prophesy and do not forbid to speak with tongues. Paul began and was ending the fourteenth chapter of 1 Corinthians with a plea to desire the spirituals from the Holy Spirit and especially to prophesy and again to desire earnestly to prophesy. Those were good words for the church at Corinth and they are even better words for us to obey today.

Chapter Review

For all may prophesy. This is a clear statement saying that prophecy is for everyone. According to Paul's writings we are to have a zeal or passion to prophesy. The term prophecy can refer a spiritual gift or a grace gift and there is also a spirit of prophecy when Jesus is talked about, preached about and shared with others. Prophecy may be simple to edify, exhort and comfort or it may be compound with another spiritual along with the prophecy. No matter what specific type of prophecy, the purpose and result are similar in the end.

Chapter Ten: Prophecy

When Paul wrote in First Corinthians fourteen to follow love, it is the picture of chasing after something of value. According to "Word Pictures in the New Testament" by A. T. Robertson Vol IV page 181 the last part of verse one is present subjective: *"that ye may keep prophesying"*. Chase after love as a prize to be obtained and desire the spirituals that you may keep prophesying. (in my words) In verse thirty-nine again the emphasis is to desire earnestly to prophesy and forbid not to speak with tongues. We are to keep prophesying. That is a bold statement and one we should take to heart.

Prophecy has an importance which has been neglected and will come again into prominence as the Holy Spirit ignites a passion in our spirits which will not be extinguished by the teaching of man or the attacks of the demonic realm. It is a vital tool to nurture the Bride of Christ in preparation of the Lord's return. It is to be a healing balm for the wounded, it is to be a flame to ignite passions which have grown cold by the rejection of the world, it is to reveal the secrets of the heart to revel in the worship of the Lord, and prophesying will open the hearts for healing of many Christians who have suffered deep spiritual wounds at the hands and the words of their brothers and sisters in Christ.

Paul wrote in Romans 11:29; *"For the gifts and calling of God are irrevocable"*. Now, the direct reference is to the nation of Israel but the truth of the statement may be applied to many areas as well. To apply it to the spirituals and also to the call of God in our lives does not violate the sanctity of what is written or be outside the character of God. A dozen verses later Paul writes about gifts and using them in proportion to our faith. Which brings an interesting question for us to consider; If we are to desire the spirituals and especially to prophesy are we responsible for the developing of our gifts to fulfill the call of the Lord?

 Paul used the word desire at the end of chapter twelve and twice in chapter fourteen. The word *zeloo* is the base of our word zealous, to be eager or have a passion, and be fervent. Are these verses just for our reading pleasure or are they verses which should burn into our spirits and souls until there is no escaping the truth brought to our understanding? If I remember an English lesson on sentence structure when there is not a subject listed YOU are the subject. But you earnestly desire the best gifts. You pursue love and desire spiritual gifts, but especially that you may prophesy. Therefore brethren, you desire earnestly to prophesy and do not forbid to speak with tongues. There is a personal responsibility to believe and take action on and from the word of God.

How many Christians will stand at the judgment seat of Christ where their works are judged by fire and find we neglected to do many things the Word of God reveals to us. I understand there are many churches and denominations which do not believe the gifts or the spiritual gifts are for today. The reasoning is the gifts were to establish the church and once the church was established there was no further need for the gifts. That sounds like a logical explanation that someone could use to justify not seeking after the gifts. I do not find that reason in the Bible for not seeking and desiring the gifts. How is it possible to take out the admonitions of Paul in first Corinthians and elsewhere in the Word of God and say that was only for this time period? Why just decide the gifts were no longer necessary? How about the resurrection or the Lord's return? That last statement seems ridiculous, which is exactly my point on not seeking and desiring to have the gifts or spirituals function in our lives.

Are we responsible for our obedience to the teaching of the Word of God? If we are, and I believe we are, then we also have a responsibility to allow the gifts to operate and function in our lives. Not only do we have a responsibility to seek the gifts and especially to keep on prophesying. We should know that the heart of the Father and our Lord is to be able to love others through the operation of the gifts in our lives.

Prophecy and prophesying are light to a darkened spiritual world and to us individually. When the light of the Lord's word and His love flows into a person receiving prophecy and their face begins to shine and you see a spark in their eyes it is assurance that the love of the Father has reached into their lives. Prophesying may bring healing to a person in a variety of ways. Prophecies may help aid in your warfare as Paul wrote to Timothy. He also wrote so Timothy would stir up the gift in him which was given by prophecy and the laying on of hands. Paul wrote those words to Timothy because prophecy was a vital functioning gift giving encouragement to the young pastor. We need this gift of prophecy to function with the power of the Holy Spirit to edify, exhort and comfort. It is our responsibility to yield ourselves as willing vessels.

Prophecy is rhema. It is the spoken life giving word. Logos is the written word. Some scholars disagree and those who are not charismatic or Pentecostal object the most. I am stating it here for clarification. The Greeks used rhema to mean utterance or what was spoken. In Ephesians 6:17 we are to take the sword of the Spirit which is the word (Rhema) of God. The sword works when it is spoken as Jesus used rhema by quoting from the Word of God when tempted by Satan.

Prophecy may have an element of personal responsibility. Paul wrote to Timothy about stirring up the gift and to not neglect the gift in him which was given by prophecy. Timothy had a responsibility to use, maintain and stir up what was given to him. Paul also wrote in First Thessalonians chapter five to not quench the Spirit and despise not prophesyings. We should be cautious that our actions do not dampen or limit the Holy Spirit's grace and flowing movement in our lives or fellowships. To despise is to make utterly nothing of, make contemptible, to not esteem or regard as nothing. Prophecy may be for now or in the future and we must open our hearts to accept and take action if necessary.

Prophecy is not usually a direct answer. However, a prophecy may confirm a truth to the one receiving the prophecy. It is more encouraging to be faithful and by being faithful events occur. There is usually a personal responsibility to cooperate in the fulfilling or completion of a prophecy. There is also the element of time. We tend to want our lives to be in order immediately and God chooses to work in our lives over time. When I receive a word saying the Lord sees my struggle and He will deliver me from the situation that may give the strength and encouragement I need but it doesn't bring deliverance at that moment. A prophecy may lift you and enable you to grow as the Lord desires. Because a prophecy doesn't happen overnight does not mean it will not happen or come true.

I have a passion to write and teach about prophecy. I had a vision one day while praying before a small church gathering was to meet in our home. I was sitting in a chair positioned in a corner. I was either in the spirit or having an interactive vision. An angel stood in front of me with a sword in front of him. The point of the sword was on the carpet and he held the sword by the hilt. The angel spoke and said I am Gabriel who stands in the presence of the Lord and have come to give you this sword. I am not sure if there was or is a proper way to respond to that. My mind was churning and I thought this is Gabriel; the Gabriel who appeared unto Daniel, unto Zacharias and unto Mary. I must be going crazy why would Gabriel be standing in front of me? I must be losing my ability to think.

The verse about trying the spirits came into my mind and I said, whether aloud or silently I do not remember, "Confess that Jesus has come in the flesh". Gabriel was immediately in a position where his right knee was on the floor, his left elbow was on his left knee and he bowed with his head down and said, "My Lord and my God," as Jesus was entering the front door which was to my right. I thought, oh my, I should listen to what he has to say. Immediately he was standing and holding the sword again but this time he was holding it by the hilt with his left hand and his right hand was supporting the blade. I say immediately because no movement was seen. He said, "I am to give you this sword."

I replied, "I am not sure what this means and how I am to use this sword". The angel replied, "It will be revealed unto you in due time." I took the sword with my right hand on the hilt and my left hand supporting the blade. It was a big sword, too big to use in the flesh. It had an ornate gold hilt at least that was the color I remember. It is a two edged sword tapering down to a point. I say it was big because from the floor it came up to my throat. The angel, Gabriel was gone as I was viewing the sword. I am not sure how I would describe Gabriel because of the overwhelming sense that what was happening was of such magnitude I wondered if it was real. I was trying to test the spirit and know it was real; I never focused on what his appearance was like.

I prayed over this vision for a long time. It was many years later when I was writing, "Let the Living Waters Flow" that I felt a stirring in my spirit and a voice speaking to me saying. This is your rhema; to speak, teach, and learn about prophecy. I am not sure that is theologically correct as I haven't heard much if any teaching on rhema being used in this manner.

It wasn't long after that I visited a house church and the pastor asked if I had anything I would like to share with the people. I again had a vision which was strange to my understanding. I saw myself in caricature or almost like a cartoon. In this form when I was asked to speak I pulled open my chest like Clark Kent would do as he was changing clothes and revealing the big S on his chest for superman. No, I don't have a big S on my chest. When I pulled my chest apart I took hold of the hilt of the sword the angel Gabriel had given to me which was inside me and brought it out and started speaking or prophesying to each person there. This happened multiple times when I was asked to share anything I had for people gathered in a small group setting. I believe I am to share about prophecy as part of my calling and also because of the vision. I hesitate to share this because even though I have come to believe in the experiences I have as long as they do not violate the word of God, a part of me questions why God would choose me. And, Gabriel giving me a sword sounds pretty farfetched. On the other hand I am doing what I know I must do and that is to do everything I am able to do to bring prophecy to a more active role in the body of Christ

Chapter Review

Prophecy is the spoken life giving word. Prophecy nurtures, heals, ignites passion, reveals our deep secrets lost to us, and can open our hearts to the Love of Christ. Just as Timothy did, we have a responsibility to stir up, use and maintain the gift of prophecy in our lives.

A prophecy may lift you and enable you to grow as the Lord desires. We are to not despise prophecy, however, we may need to pray about it and see what God can bring to pass in our lives with our willingness to grow. Prophecy may take time to reach fruition in our lives.

Chapter Eleven: Revelation Gifts

Different kinds of tongues, the interpretation of tongues and prophecy are vocal gifts. They are speaking under the anointing of the Holy Spirit to edify, exhort and comfort. Without speaking these gifts do not function. The next group of three I am going to expound upon is the discerning of spirits, the word of knowledge, and the word of wisdom. These are revelation manifestations in that all require a revelation and insight from the Holy Spirit which is beyond the knowledge or insight from our natural understanding, intelligence, or the natural ability of the soul.

Discerning of spirits is exactly what is implied; it is the ability to discern the spiritual manifestation of angels, demons or the spirits of men. It is not the gift of discernment whereby any type of judgment may be issued against a person or situation. Now, sometimes the Holy Spirit might reveal the cause of a situation but that would be a word of knowledge.

The discerning of spirits may operate or function through many avenues of expression. One may perceive an odor of sulfur or rotting garbage and know there is an unclean spirit involved. Another may see a vision or a picture flash through their mind revealing the spirit involved. Color is another way the gift may function; seeing a darkness is indicative of an evil spirit. It may function with a sense or feeling which could be a person's spirit being prompted to be aware of spiritual forces at work. The Holy Spirit uses varied ways to reveal to a person what is transpiring in the spirit world. Another way might be a vision or daydream or even a night vision or dream. For others it is an opening of spiritual eyes and they see what is in the spirit world. Regardless of the method, it is the Holy Spirit making known what spirit is involved.

"Now it happened, as we went to prayer, that a certain slave girl possessed with a spirit of divination met us, who brought her masters much profit by fortune-telling. This girl followed Paul and us, and cried out, saying, 'These men are the servants of the Most High God, who proclaim to us the way of salvation.' And this she did for many days. But Paul, greatly annoyed, turned and said to the spirit, "I command you in the name of Jesus Christ to come out of her." And he came out

that very hour. (Acts 16:16-18) Paul became annoyed by the presence of this spirit which was a revealing of the spiritual force using this slave girl.

*"And when the servant of the man of God arose early and went out, there was an army, surrounding the city with horses and chariots. And his servant said to him, "Alas my master! What shall we do?" So he answered, "Do not fear, for those who are with us are more than those who are with them." And Elisha prayed, and said, "Lord, I pray, open his eyes that he may see." Then the Lord opened the eyes of the young man, and he saw. And behold, the mountain was full of horses and chariots of fire all around Elish*a." (2 Kings 15:15-17) To have your eyes opened and see into the spiritual realm is one avenue which manifests the discerning of spirits. Elisha's servant saw an angelic host surrounding them.

I was talking to a friend about the Lord and answering the questions he voiced about religion. As I was speaking to him I felt my eyes rolled over and I was seeing in both the natural and spirit. I saw a small demonic creature with its hand inside his head. This spirit had a realization that I could see him and tried to hide behind the persons head. I spoke from my spirit and said, "In the name of Jesus you must leave." It disappeared. The person with whom I was talking shook his head from side to side and said, "I don't know what just happened but I had a terrible headache all day and it just left."

Seeing into the spiritual realm unveils the plan, intent and even the appearance of angelic or demonic forces. What is seen is revealed by the Holy Spirit. There are a variety of classes of spirits as Paul wrote in Ephesians 6:12: *"For we do not wrestle against flesh and blood, but against principalities, against powers, against the rulers of the darkness of this age, against spiritual hosts of wickedness in the heavenly places."* I believe there are many classes which are not mentioned in scripture. I am saying this because when I look at illustrations for some comic books, movies and even some tattoos I see copies of what I have seen in the spirit world. They are real and would like to steal, kill and destroy your life. What I see reveals their influence is growing and their appearance is accepted by those who either willingly or unknowingly are advertising for the spirit world. I pray the church awakens to the darkness around and the discerning of spirits would become normal as a tool to rise against the onslaught becoming available through so many media. Even though the demonic spirit world is real and they do have a certain level of power, greater is He who is in us than he who is in the world. I can overcome the enemy as I am in Christ. Without His power and authority we would be helpless.

A word of knowledge is a small piece of the knowledge of the Lord given by the Holy Spirit. It is a supernatural insight into a situation, circumstance or even events in a person's life. It is something which is not known by human understanding.

"Then one of them, named Agabus, stood up and showed by the Spirit that there was going to be a great famine throughout all the world, which also happened in days of Claudius Caesar." (Acts 11:28)

"And as we stayed many days, a certain prophet named Agabus came down from Judea. When he had come to us, he took Paul's belt, bound his own hands and feet, and said, 'Thus says the Holy Spirit, So shall the Jews at Jerusalem bind the man who owns this belt, and deliver him into the hands of the Gentiles." (Acts 21:10,11)

Agabus is identified as a prophet through whom the Holy Spirit enabled this gift, the word of knowledge, to function. He stood and spoke of a famine which was to come. That was a piece or snippet of knowledge known only to the Lord until it was revealed through Agabus. Next he used a visual demonstration and spoke according to the Holy Spirit and explained the object lesson of binding his own hands and feet. There are those who would define this as a personal prophecy. However, I do not agree but, even if it was, it is still the Holy Spirit at work. Through our human understanding we may misinterpret or disagree on terminology.

I will not relate the whole story here of Jesus and the woman at the well from the fourth chapter of the gospel of John. He said to her go call your husband. She said I have no husband. Jesus said that is rightly spoken you have had five husbands and the one you are with now is not your husband. Jesus spoke to her by having a word of knowledge given to Him by the Holy Spirit. When Agabus spoke of the famine and the knowledge of Paul being bound he did not give direction on what to do in either situation. A decision was made by a council to send relief in response to the word of knowledge. It is not always revealed what our personal response should or could be. It is just revealing a portion of knowledge. It may require prayer and council before any action is taken. When Agabus spoke of Paul being bound those around begged him not to go to Jerusalem. Paul didn't heed their pleas. It might have been given to prepare Paul for what lie ahead. The knowledge revealed might have caused all who knew what awaited Paul to pray for his protection as he was going to Jerusalem.

The word of knowledge and the word of wisdom often come side by side to work together. When Peter had a vision in Acts chapter ten he was thinking about it when the Spirit said to him, "*Behold, three men are seeking you. Arise therefore, go down and go with them doubting nothing for I have sent them.*" Peter received a word of knowledge: three men are seeking you. He then received a word of wisdom with instructions on what to do with the word of knowledge: go with them without doubting for I have sent them. When Cornelius received a vision he was told his prayers and giving had come before the Lord. That was a word of knowledge given by an angel in a vision. Next he was told what to do; he sent men to Joppa to the very house where peter was staying. He had a word of wisdom to know what to do and another word of knowledge to find Peter's lodging.

God spoke to Noah and said there would be a great flood. That was a piece of God's knowledge. He was also instructed to build an ark. He had a direction or ministry and probably received numerous words of knowledge to aid in the building of the ark. Then the Lord had Noah go inside while God sealed the ark.

Elisha spoke a word of wisdom for Naaman to go dip seven times in the river Jordan. His servant Gehazi followed Naaman after Elisha had refused a gift for his services and lied to get money and clothes. When he returned Elisha said, "*Did not my spirit go with you.*" It was a word of knowledge which revealed to Elisha the actions of his servant. The word of wisdom reveals Naaman's leprosy would now come upon Gehazi.

I was with a friend and we were asking God to use us and I received a word of knowledge about a town, a street, a house number and a name of the person who lived there. We decided to drive to that town and try to find the street, house, and person. Much to my surprise we found the street easily; it was not a common street name like elm or main. We drove past the street, turned around and went back and started driving looking for a house number. There it was. I told him to park and I went to the door and asked for the person. I was thinking it was just my imagination but a lady said he just went to the store and would be back in about ten minutes. I said that we would come back later. I was probably as shocked as I could be. We prayed and went back and ministered to a young man.

 A word of wisdom may be the action taken based upon the word of knowledge. Direction may be given by a word of wisdom which is not preceded by a word of knowledge. I have found they usually are paired together. Paul had a dream where a man from Macedonia was asking Paul to come help. Paul concluded it was a call to Macedonia.

Discerning of Spirits is a supernatural power to detect, know or see into the realm of spirits and their activities. It may work hand in hand with a word of knowledge or a word of wisdom to have a supernatural revelation of the enemy's plans and purpose and how to war against those plans or purposes. It is not the natural discernment which comes by growth and maturity as mentioned in Hebrews 5:12.

A word of knowledge is a revelation of knowledge not known by natural avenues. It may concern the divine will of God. It may be facts which when known give an insight otherwise unknown. A word of knowledge may stand alone or may work in conjunction with Discerning of Spirits or a Word of Wisdom.

A Word of Wisdom gives perspective or direction for accomplishing the will of God. It may give personal understanding as to a course of action either for an individual or a church. Again it may function alone but also works with a Word of Knowledge and Discerning of Spirits.

Chapter Review

The revelation gifts are the revealing of what is not known by human understanding, reasoning or ability but are divine insights from the Holy Spirit.

Discerning of Spirits is a revealing of the spiritual forces at work in a person, place or events. The gift may operate so we command the evil spirits to leave. It may operate with a word of knowledge or a word of wisdom so we pray, proclaim and declare freedom from oppressing spirits in a person's life or a situation.

A word of knowledge is a small piece of God's knowledge revealed to us by the Holy Spirit to have us pray for a person or situation. It may be a revealing of the plan and purposes of the Lord concerning an area of our lives or someone else's life. It is factual and is information which we may pray about and discern what our response should be to what is revealed.

A word of wisdom may lead us to know what action we should pursue concerning a word of knowledge or discerning of spirits. A word of wisdom may reveal divine direction. It may also reveal the plan of the Lord for an individual or a fellowship.

Chapter Twelve: Power Gifts

The gift of Faith, the Gifts of Healings and the Working of Miracles are known as power gifts. They each demonstrate an aspect of the power of God. In our nation's history President Gerald Ford pardoned former President Richard Nixon from his involvement in the Watergate scandal. That was possible because of the law of executive clemency stating the president may pardon someone for the interest of national security or for the good of the nation. The president had the power to suspend the law in that special instance. God has executive clemency over all the natural laws of the universe. When He uses the Holy Spirit to suspend a natural law it allows for a miracle or healing take place.

The gift of Faith is difficult to identify clearly because it almost never stands alone. Faith may bring about the Working of Miracles or the Gifts of Healings. The missionary journeys of Paul, though anointed and sent by the church at Antioch were probably a manifestation of the Gift of Faith. He had the ability to believe God without any doubt. This Faith may be the sustaining factor when facing adverse circumstance and staying strong in the witness and perseverance to achieve the Lord's will in a person's life.

When Daniel was put into the den of lions it was because he continued his daily ritual of prayer after the edict from the king that made it illegal to ask a petition of any god. He prayed three times daily knowing he would be thrown into the den of lions. Daniel survived a night in the midst of a large number of hungry lions. Later all the people who had the King sign a decree were cast into the same den along with their families; all their bones were broken before they reached the bottom. I have often wondered if Daniel used a lion as a pillow. If he did, it was possible by the Gift of Faith.

A church I was attending was launching a television station in northern Indiana. It is TV 63 today but there were many problems facing the erection of a tower for the signal to be transmitted and much prayer and fasting was asked for and received during this long struggle to bring the station to reality. Every time I heard a request for prayer and fasting I felt a gentle prompting from the Holy Spirit to not pray for the tower to be built. Instead I was to pray for the workers who would be hired to work the station and control the programming and everything necessary for the station to run smoothly. I knew the station would be a reality through the gift of Faith. There was never any doubt in my mind and I continued to pray according to the divine direction I was given.

In 1 Kings Seventeen Elijah went to a widow of Zarephath whom the Lord ordained to provide for him. He asked for a drink and then asked for a little bread. The widow said she only had a little and she was gathering wood to fix a last meal for her and her son and then they would die. Elijah said, *"For thus says the Lord God of Israel: 'the bin of flour shall not be used up, nor shall the jar of oil run dry, until the day the Lord sends rain on the earth.'"* (Verse 14) It is possible what she had saved for a last meal fed three people for years. That was faith in the Word of the Lord and it was put into action. It might have also been a Working of Miracles combined with Faith.

When her son died Elijah prayed over the child and his soul came back to him. Death is something which only the supernatural gift of Faith can conquer. Jesus told Lazarus to come forth out of the tomb he was in. The gift of Faith will cause life to come to dead bodies. The gift of Faith will cause lions to not bite and devour you. It might also cause iron to swim to the top of a stream. (2 Kings 6:6)

The working of miracles may best be illustrated by Jesus turning water into wine. It was not only transformed into wine but it was very good wine.

"And when they ran out of wine, the mother of Jesus said to Him, 'They have no wine.' Jesus said to her, 'Woman, what does your concern have to do with me? My hour has not yet come.' His mother said to the servants, 'Whatever He says to you do it.' Now there were set there six waterpots of stone according to the manner of purification of the Jews, containing twenty or thirty gallons apiece. Jesus said to them, 'Fill the waterpots with water. ' And they filled them up to the brim. And He said to them, *'Draw some out now and take it the master of the feast.' And they took it. When the master of the feast had tasted the water that was made wine, and did not know where it came from (but the servants who had drawn the water knew), the master of the feast called the bridegroom. And he said to him, 'Every man at the beginning sets out the good wine, and when the guest have well drunk, the inferior. You have kept the good wine until now.'"* (John 2:3-10)

Another example occurs in 2 Kings 2:8. *"Now Elijah took his mantle, rolled it up and struck the water, and it was divided this way and that, so that the two of them crossed over on dry ground."* To take a coat and hit the river Jordan so it not only divided but the ground dried so they crossed on dry ground is indeed a miracle. Later when Elijah was taken to heaven by a whirlwind Elisha went back to the river Jordan. *"He also took up the mantle of Elijah that had fallen from him and went back and stood by the bank of the Jordan. Then he took the mantle of Elijah that had fallen from him, and struck the water and said, 'Where is the Lord God of Elijah?' And when he also struck the water, it was divided this way and that; and Elisha crossed over."* (2 Kings 2: 13, 14)

"A certain woman of the wives of the sons of the prophets cried out to Elisha, saying, 'Your servant my husband is dead, and you know that your servant feared the Lord. And the creditor is coming to take my two sons to be his slaves.' So Elisha said to her, 'What shall I do for you? Tell me what do you have in the house?' And she said, 'Your maidservant has nothing in the house but a jar of oil.' Then he said, 'Go, borrow vessels from everywhere, from all your neighbors—empty vessels; do not gather just a few. And when you have come in, you shall shut the door behind you and your sons; then pour it into all those vessels, and set aside the full ones.' So, she went from him and shut the door behind her and her sons, who brought the vessels to her; and she poured it out. Now it came to pass, when the vessels were full, that she said to her son, 'Bring me another vessel.' And he said to her, 'There is not another vessel.' So the oil ceased. Then she came and told the man of God. And he said, 'Go, sell the oil and pay your debt, and you and your sons live on the rest." (2 Kings 4: 1-7)

Elisha had a Word of Wisdom to know what to do with a single jar of oil. When the widow and her sons obeyed a miracle occurred. Have you ever wondered how many miracles are missed because to do what seems improbable leads to the impossible happening. It is also possible that the Gift of Faith was operating in Elisha and he knew the outcome of their obedience.

The Gifts of Healings is the supernatural working of the Holy Spirit to bring healing or cures to a variety of sickness. The word Gifts is plural showing there are many gifts and ways they function. The word healings is also plural showing a variety of healings. In the translation of the New Testament there are three main words which are all translated heal or healing. The meanings and the Greek words are taken from Strong's Exhaustive Concordance.

The first is *therapeuo* meaning to relieve of disease, cure or heal. It is the word translated most often. In Mt. 12:15 it is the word used when it states that Jesus healed them all. It is also used in verse 22 when he healed a demon-possessed, blind and mute man. We have the word therapy from the root of this Greek word.

The next word is *iaomai* which means to cure, heal or make whole. It is used when Jesus touched the ear of the servant of the high priest and restored his ear in Lk. 22:51. It is the word used in this story. *"Now when Jesus had entered Capernaum, a centurion came to Him, pleading with Him, saying, 'Lord my servant is lying at home paralyzed, dreadfully tormented...Then Jesus said to the centurion. 'Go your way; and as you have believed, so let it be done for you.' And his servant was healed that same hour."*

The third word is *sozo*, with the meaning to save, deliver, protect, heal, preserve or make whole. It is used in Lk. 8:36 when telling that the man with the legion of demons was healed. It is used in Acts 14 when Paul was in Lystra and spoke to the man who was without strength in his legs and was a cripple from his mother's womb. When Paul observed him intently and seeing he had faith to be healed told him to stand up straight on his feet. And he leaped and walked.

There is some commonality between the words and different words were sometimes used when the circumstances are similar and it shows, regardless of the word which was translated, it is the Gifts of Healings in operation. At times a person was told to do something; i.e. take up your bed and walk, go wash your eyes or dip in the river Jordan. Healing may not be automatic but might occur over time and it may require action on the part of the person receiving. To ask a man who had never stood on his feet to stand straight seems like an impossible statement. By doing so the person receiving the healings would know immediately they were healed.

The spirituals are the Gifts of the Holy Spirit. As part of the sovereign Trinity the Holy Spirit in His working may blend many of the Gifts to bring about the desired result. As such occurs we should not be overly concerned if it was a Working of Miracles or Gifts of Healings. It is the result of His gifting that one is healed, cured, delivered or maybe all three aspects were necessary for one to be made whole. Whether it was by the Gift of Faith, the Working of Miracles or the Gifts of Healings we may not have the understanding to discern which was more predominate. It really doesn't matter. The explanation of the Spirituals is to give our finite minds a glimpse into the majestic, awesome power of the Holy Spirit. By desiring the Spirituals and seeking to allow the Lord to love others through our obedience the power promised to those who believe is brought into reality through the Spirituals.

Chapter Review

The Gift of Faith is more than our normal faith. It may operate along with the working of miracles and the gifts of healings. It is a supernatural impartation of faith to believe and bring about the impossible.

Chapter Thirteen: Led by the Spirit

How do you walk so the spirituals are a part of your life? We walk by faith and not by sight and the just shall live by faith. We need to walk according to the Spirit. For as many as are led by the Spirit of God, these are the sons of God. Paul wrote in Ephesians 4:1, *"I therefore, the prisoner of the Lord beseech you to walk worthy of the calling with which you are called."* The apostle John in his epistle wrote we are to walk in love as Paul also wrote in Ephesians. Over twenty five times in the New Testament are we not admonished to walk in truth, love, and to walk worthy of the calling. The word walk is not telling us to take a walk around the block but is referring to a lifestyle of obedience.

How did Peter know he was to answer the crowd which gathered at Pentecost? How did he know to reach out and lift the cripple as he and John were going to the temple to pray? What did he feel during these encounters? We do not know. We do know he was led by the Holy Spirit. It will not be any different for our lives as it was for Peter, John, Phillip and Paul. We also must be led by the Holy Spirit. There is not a manual to tell you what to think and how you will feel when the Holy Spirit desires to flow through you to love someone through the spirituals.

Our relationship with the Lord is a combination of obedience and faith. There are supernatural influences upon our lives. Our lives are a combination of what is natural and physical and what is Holy and supernatural. We have the grace of God in our lives which brings about transformation from the carnal to the spiritual at salvation and continues manifesting grace throughout our lives. It is truly a unique and wonderful relationship. As awesome as this is it does not give individual guidance as to how and where the spirituals will function in our lives. How will we know what to do? We have no choice but to yield to the Holy Spirit and walk by faith.

We do, however, have some advantages over the apostles. We have the word of God and we have the experiences of the apostles in the early church recorded in the book of Acts. Although we will not gain the knowledge of how the spirituals will function in our individual lives and how each one may learn to be led by the Holy Spirit we will gain understanding of how the Holy Spirit leads by taking a look at those experiences in the book of Acts. Though some of these may not seem to be supernatural leadings they are practical steps and the practical blends with the supernatural.

Jesus commanded the disciples to not depart from Jerusalem but to wait for the promise of the Father and they would be baptized with the Holy Spirit. The first aspect is to be obedient. Imagine what might have happened if the one hundred and twenty who met in the upper room had each went their own way? Obedience in our lives should be primary and continuous. They continued with one accord in prayer and supplication on the Day of Pentecost. Obedience is the first step of a lifetime journey.

The second aspect we see is prayer. Their prayer was in harmony and agreement. Both aspects are important. Prayer is a dynamic force, a catalyst to bring the supernatural into the natural and it is both a spiritual tool and the way to communicate with the Father, Son and Holy Spirit. They were in agreement and unity. They may not have prayed exactly the same way or with the same words but their spirits were united together for a common cause.

The third aspect is unity. No one functions in the body of Christ by themselves. I was having breakfast with a co-worker and he asked about my being a minister and in the conversation I asked about his relationship with the Lord. He said he felt he could worship and follow God at his breakfast nook as well as going to a fellowship gathering. I asked him what songs were sung for worship and what he learned from the Bible the previous week. He just looked at me with a blank stare. I asked him to lay his hand flat on the table between us. I took out a pocket knife with a five inch blade and placed my hand on his to hold it in position. I placed the knife near his little finger and asked if he would mind if I cut off a quarter inch of his finger. He wondered if I was serious. I said I was and his hand pulled back and went under the table. I asked, "Do you think that section of your finger would do well if I cut it off from your body?" He said I see what you are saying; I will find a place to go. We are the body of Christ; we will not survive on our own. The body functions in unity and harmony and the body does what is necessary to maintain itself. Unity.

On the Day of Pentecost every believer accepted what the Holy Spirit brought to them. No one said it wasn't what they expected. The other apostles didn't argue because Peter stood and shared. They all continued in the apostle's doctrine, fellowship, breaking of bread and prayers.

The fourth aspect is continuing. The accepting of the provision of the Lord for salvation and growing in grace and walking in the Spirit is a lifetime agreement and is to be continued for a lifetime. One prayer we should all consider praying is for a return to active fellowship of those who willingly or by the attacks of the enemy are abiding without the body. We are the body. We function better with all the parts of our body.

They had a joy and gladness and simplicity of heart and were praising God and having favor with all the people. The fifth aspect of being led by the Spirit is joy and gladness. The joy of the Lord is our strength. We could choose to ignore all the Lord has provided and rely on our feelings. Our feelings change with each circumstance but our joy is based on the Lord and the promises of His Word. Praise from a joyful heart indicates we believe He is in control and we should believe what is written and rejoice. This life is but for a moment and eternity is unfathomable and forever.

The sixth aspect is praising God. Praising God releases a spiritual breakthrough from heaven to earth. There are almost three hundred verses which tell of praise or praising. The Lord resides in the praises of His people. Praise is a powerful gift we have been given.

Peter and John were going to the temple to pray and said to a beggar look on us. The custom was for a beggar to not look upon others, so he expected to receive something when Peter said look on us and he received more than expected. The seventh aspect is to be open and ready when going about your daily routine. They were going to pray which was part of their daily activity and when the opportunity arose they responded by being sensitive to the Holy Spirit. A man who had never walked not only walked but leaped and praised the Lord. It is being sensitive in daily routines when someone is encountered who needs a manifestation of the love of God through a spiritual gift. The man was not in a healing crusade or a miracle convention he was where his life was at the time; a beggar looking for help.

Peter and John were put in custody and questioned about the miracle. The eighth aspect is to have a steadfast boldness. They had a steadfast boldness to continue sharing about Jesus and what He does in beggar's lives even when the religious system told them not to speak about Jesus. They prayed for a boldness to speak His word.

The ninth aspect is to be honest in the things you do and be sensitive to when the Holy Spirit guides you into truth. In Acts chapter five, Ananias and Sapphira lost their lives by not being honest. Peter was sensitive to the Holy Spirit and asked them about their dealings which gave them an opportunity to be honest and live.

The tenth aspect is after this happened many more believers were added and the ministry exploded. Great healings and deliverances occurred so even the shadow of Peter brought deliverance. There was a step by step process to bring the apostles and early church to where the ministry exploded. After the apostles were thrown into prison an angel came and delivered them. This is not an aspect of being led by the Spirit but when we are led by the Spirit miraculous things happen even being set free from prison.

I have shared ten aspects of being led by the Spirit in the first five chapters of Acts. In chapter six there is a controversy. Number eleven is that with growth comes controversy. How we handle controversy determines our progress. Here the apostles said to the people you decide on this one. Choose seven men of good reputation, full of the Holy Spirit and wisdom. Sometimes we do not have to handle the conflict but give direction to others. Because of this the word spread and the disciples multiplied.

Having others help in serving is the twelfth aspect. Deacons were appointed to minister to the needs of the Greek widows and for those obedient in serving greater ministry were given. Stephen was full of the Holy Spirit and did great signs and wonders. Each person has a responsibility to minister to one another and to serve one another.

Philip, one of the seven deacons, went to Samaria and preached and a great many were saved. Then an angel of the Lord spoke to him and said take a walk to the south toward Gaza. He wasn't told how far he might have to walk as Gaza was a hundred plus miles away. If an angel told you to take a hundred mile walk would you go? The thirteenth aspect of being led is becoming aware the spirit realm may open in new ways while we are walking by faith. After baptizing the eunuch from Ethiopia he disappeared and appeared in another town.

The fourteenth aspect of being led by the Spirit is doing what may cause concern or apprehension in you. Ananias was instructed of the Lord in a vision to go pray for the man who was destroying Christians and having them put in jail. He was obedient and prayed for Saul to receive his sight and the Holy Spirit. I wonder if he questioned the Lord. Maybe he thought this needs to be from the Lord or I might be thrown in jail or lose my life.

The fifteenth aspect is shown by Barnabas who took Paul and interceded for him to the other leaders so they would accept him and his work. We need the help of others. Our approval, support and acknowledging of others may be the catalyst necessary for them to grow and become all they are called to be. What if Barnabas hadn't interceded on Paul's behalf? How might the ministry of Paul differed and would he have remained outside the fellowship of others?

The sixteenth aspect is Peter traveled through the country and continued healing and raising the dead. It mentions no other apostle or traveling companion. Are we willing to stand and travel alone to do the work of the Lord? This was possibly a short season in the life of Peter. We all may have a season when we have to stand or work alone.

Barnabas heard what was happening in Antioch and had to go see for himself. After being there he decided to go find Paul and together they taught for a year in Antioch where believers were first called Christians. The seventeenth aspect seems to be opposite of the previous aspect. We need to be able to stand alone when necessary and also be wise enough to enlist help when necessary.

The eighteenth aspect is listening and obeying those who have spiritual authority. The Holy Spirit spoke to a group of prophets and said separate Barnabas and Paul for the work I have called them to. They fasted and prayed, laid hands on them and sent them on their way. This was not one person in charge but a group. Abuses come when one person believes they are the authority. God confirms and assures His children of His messages and callings. There is a tier of spiritual authority within the church not to rule over others but to guide and serve the body for growth.

The nineteenth aspect is that they met Elymas the sorcerer. The enemy will have someone who opposes what you are doing so be prepared for the attacks of the enemy. Some form of persecution or resistance from those we try to help may also occur. The enemy tries to keep people in spiritual darkness and will resist the attempts to bring light into their world.

The twentieth aspect is to be careful not to accept adulation which exalts you. Paul and Silas were thought to be gods and the people wanted to worship them. (Acts 14:11-13) There is a world of difference between being honored as a servant and being exalted. Spiritual people will honor you for what you are doing. Carnal people will exalt you. We should learn to honor those who are worthy of honor. We should strive to be worthy of honor with humility knowing it is the Lord working in and through us.

The twenty-first aspect is just doing what seems good. *"However, it seemed good to Silas to remain there."* (Acts 15:34) In the King James Version it is written it pleased Silas to remain there. No great leading, no voice from heaven, no angel telling him to stay, not even a vision he just felt he was supposed to stay. Shortly thereafter Paul and Barnabas had a disagreement over John Mark and Paul chose Silas to go with him on his further travels. By doing what seemed good he was in the right place at the right time.

The twenty-second aspect is sometimes our plans are not the Holy Spirit's plans. "Now when they had gone through Phrygia and the region of Galatia, they were forbidden by the Holy Spirit to preach the word in Asia. After they had come to Mysis they tried to go into Bithynia, but the Spirit did not permit them." (Acts 16:7, 8) Learning to not go where we are not led is an important lesson.

The twenty-third aspect of being led by the Spirit is to be sensitive and understand dreams and visions. (For further study on dreams and visions I suggest reading "The Seer" by James W Goll) A vision of a man of Macedonia came to Paul in the night. The man pleaded for him to come to Macedonia. Paul took action but the context suggests he and Silas discussed it first.

The twenty-fourth aspect of being led by the Spirit is receiving the protection and provision from others. An angry mob came from Thessalonica to stir up crowds against Paul. Paul was protected by friends and escorted away to Athens. Our lives may or may not be threatened with the loss of our life for serving Jesus. We might not need that protection and provision to live. Each of us will have times of distress, turmoil and trials when we need others to be there and provide what is necessary for us to be victorious.

The twenty-fifth aspect is having your spirit stirred or provoked by the Holy Spirit. At Athens Paul was moved by seeing the city given over to idols. Exactly what Paul felt the word doesn't say but it prompted him to action. We know the world around us is preparing for the return of the Lord? This alone should stir us to lay aside the cares of this world and fervently serve the Lord and others.

The twenty-sixth aspect is using common ground to relate to others. Paul saw an altar to the unknown god and he used that to preach Jesus. Being able to relate to others where they are opens many doors to minister.

The twenty-seventh aspect is do not be afraid to work as you minister. Aquila and his wife Priscilla were tent makers. Paul stayed, worked with them and continued preaching. I realize the structure of many churches prohibits a minster from doing more than caring for the people. We should be willing to work if the Lord leads and the opportunity is there. It may be just helping someone for a few hours.

The twenty-eighth aspect is receiving encouragement from the Lord. Again, in a vision the Lord instructed Paul to stay at Corinth and no one would attack or hurt him. When we serve the Lord, the insight, encouragement and direction of the Holy Spirit is vital to strengthen us to continue and to know where we are and where we should be.

The twenty-ninth aspect is to continue helping others to receive the baptism of the Holy Spirit. Paul traveled to Ephesus and found some disciples who were still following John's baptism so he told them about Christ and prayed with them to receive the Holy Spirit. Paul had great visions, revelations and spiritual insight which allowed him to write almost half the New Testament. He could still relate to those who were just beginning their walk with the Lord or those who had not received the baptism of the Holy Spirit. We are never too spiritual to meet the needs of others where they are in their journey.

The thirtieth aspect is in Acts 20 and verse thirty-five. The last part of the verse contains this; *"And remember the words of the Lord Jesus, that He said, 'It is more blessed to give than to receive.'"* Being led by the Spirit should cultivate in us the ability and desire to give. We should give more honor than we receive. We should give more grace than we receive. We should give more love than we receive. We should give more thanks than we receive.

These are thirty examples from the book of Acts. They are by no means all that are in the book but should serve as examples to teach us the variety of ways we are led by the Holy Spirit. It is a combination of the natural and supernatural. It is a walk of faith with sensitivity to however the Spirit leads. It is trial and error. We will not always be in perfect alignment because we are human and make mistakes. We should always be striving to be in harmony with what the Holy Spirit is striving to do. Being a willing vessel of the Holy Spirit so the spirituals and the love of the Father may flow through us and touch the hurting lives around us is a step by step process of growing. It begins when we develop a passion and zeal for the gifts and refuse to settle for anything less than the best the Lord has for us in our lives.

Though some may see me as a fanatic, or something else, I believe I am normal. I have been adopted into a family. My Father is the mighty Jehovah. He is supernatural. If there is not anything supernatural happening in my life I would question if I am part of the family. I am normal and the gifts and manifestations of the Holy Spirit are part of the family legacy. We are to be humbly guided by love, led by the Holy Spirit and seek to have the spirituals flow through us to bring the love of God into the lives of those we are in contact with.

Chapter Review

Our walk is our lifestyle of obedience. It is how we are led by the Holy Spirit. Obedience, prayer, and praising God are just some of the many aspects of being led by the spirit. We can be open and ready and bold, alone or in service with another. We can find common ground with others and possibly be a protector of another for God.

Chapter Fourteen: Led By the Spirit: Dreams and Visions

The word dream occurs over one hundred times in the Old Testament. Dreams revealed the mind of God to various people. Joseph had dreams in which he saw his brothers bowing down to him. Even though his brothers did not like the dream and sold him into slavery, the dream came to pass. Daniel revealed the dreams of Nebuchanezzer whose dreams also came to pass.

The references of dreams in the New Testament are few but those examples have significance. Joseph was admonished in a dream to not be concerned about taking Mary to be his wife for she was to birth the Son of God. He was also warned to take his wife and child and flee to Egypt and in another dream to return to Nazareth. In the Greek the word used is *onar* and refers to the natural dream process when we sleep. Another word used in Acts 2:17 is *enupniazomai* which is to dream from the root which means something seen in sleep. Dreams may reveal the sovereign will of the Lord for a person or for a nation. Dreams and visions are also a promise from the book of Joel which Peter quoted from in the second chapter of Acts verse seventeen. *"And it shall come to pass in the last days, says God. That I will pour out My Spirit on all flesh; Your sons and your daughters shall prophesy, Your young men shall see visions, Your old men shall dream dreams."* Dreams and visions are a viable means through which the Lord and the Holy Spirit reveal the will, the mind and the heart of God.

Another type of vision uses the word *horama* which according to Strong's Concordance means something gazed at; a spectacle especially something supernatural or a sight (vision). When Jesus and the disciples came down from the Mount of Transfiguration He said to tell the vision to no man until the Son of Man is risen from the dead. Matthew 17:9 In the ninth chapter of Acts both Ananias and Saul who was later called Paul received visions and instruction through visions. In the tenth chapter of Acts both Cornelius and Peter received visions. Again these carried an element of instruction with them. Cornelius was informed of where to find Peter after being instructed to send for Peter. Peter was instructed to go with the men sent from Cornelius doubting nothing. Paul had a vision of a man from Macedonia saying to come to Macedonia and help them. Acts 16:9-10. Paul concluded the Lord was calling Paul and his company to preach in Macedonia. In Acts 18:9-11 Paul had a vision of the Lord informing him to not be afraid and to preach in the city of Corinth. Paul taught there for the next eighteen months.

Another word is *horasis* which only occurs twice and has a meaning of gazing upon. It also carries the meaning of an aspect which is seen externally or an internal inspired appearance. This is used in Acts 2:17 when Peter was quoting from the prophet Joel and stated your young men shall see visions. This may mean seeing something in your mind's eye or seeing something with your spiritual eyes. It may be internal or external and may also include seeing with your physical eyes. The other reference is in Revelation 4:3 where it is translated appearance. It is something which is seen either externally or internally.

The words vision or visions occurs seventeen times in the New Testament. One word in the Greek is *optasia* which means a visuality, an apparition or vision. *Optasia* occurs first in Lk. 1:22, *"But when he came out, he could not speak to them; and they perceived that he had seen a vision in the temple, for he beckoned to them and remained speechless."* Zacharias had a vision of Gabriel who told him he would have a son who would be the forerunner of the Messiah.

In Lk 24:23, *"When they did not find His body, they came saying that they had also seen a vision of angels who said He was alive."* The two disciples on the road to Emmaus were relating the story to Jesus that the women who went to the tomb had a vision of angels saying Christ was alive.

When Paul stated in 2 Corinthians 12:1 that he would come to visions and revelations this word *optasia* is used. This word seems to be an active vision. The vision shook Zacharias; because it was so real and dynamic he had a hard time believing it. The women saw the angels who spoke to them and they told others of the experience. Paul relates the visions and revelations are how he grew in the knowledge of Christ. Seeing spiritual beings separates this type of vision from other descriptions of visions.

When Peter fell into a trance waiting for a meal to be prepared as related in the tenth chapter of the book of Acts the word is *ekstasis*. It may also be translated astonishment. It occurs in Lk 5:26; Acts 3:9-10;

Mark 16:8 and Acts 22:17-18. It might occur as a trance or the result of seeing something miraculous. I confess to a lack of understanding of this but am relating it because it is a biblical example of how the Holy Spirit may work in our lives.

Apokalupto: to reveal, to take off the cover; and *Apokalupis*: disclosure or revelation are found twenty-six and fourteen times respectively. Revelations are one of the ways the Holy Spirit guides us into truth. It is a revealing of what we might not have an understanding of or a truth in the Word of God which is what we may need at that time. The Holy Spirit is marvelous in all His ways.

The dreams and visions listed are part of the Holy Spirits leading in our lives. All the ways we are led by the Holy Spirit may be summed up when Paul wrote to the church at Galatia admonishing them to 'walk in the Spirit'. The meaning of walk according to Strong's Concordance is to tread about; walk at large (as proof of ability); to live; to follow (as a companion or votary which according to Webster is one who is bound by a vow; one devoted to a particular service, state of life, etc.) and to be occupied with.

Do we really walk according to the Spirit? I think I have much room for improvement in my walk. I am not sure how well I follow as a companion devoted to being sensitive to the Holy Spirit. At times I am more occupied with the affairs of life then the affairs of the Holy Spirit. Father, help us all to be closer to your Holy Spirit that we may truly 'walk in the Spirit.'

Chapter Review

Dreams and visions are a viable means through which the Lord and the Holy Spirit reveal the will, the mind and the heart of God. Visions can provide us with instruction or warning or reveal an understanding of truth.

Chapter Fifteen: LOVE

First Corinthians Thirteen is known as the love chapter. The word love is used nine times in the thirteen verses. The fruit of the Spirit mentioned in Galatians chapter five and verses twenty-one and twenty two has nine graces and there are nine spirituals. It is a divine occurrence. Paul says that if he speaks with the tongues on men and of angels and has not love he is making noise as an empty echo or loud clanging. If he has prophecy, understanding, knowledge, and faith to move mountains but if he doesn't have love he is nothing. He says if he gave everything away and sacrificed his body and did it without love it has no profit; it is nothing. Paul refers to spirituals in the first two verses and sacrifice in the third verse. Everything without love as the motivating and sustaining factor has no value. The last verse in chapter twelve Paul reminds us to desire the greater gifts and yet he would show a supremely excellent way. In order to gain the greater gifts we must have love.

Paul uses *agape* here for the word love. Though the word occurs in Greek writings it came to be used to signify Christian love and God's love for His children. Love suffers long and is kind. Love has staying power and passion to continue with kindness, usefulness and graciousness. Love is gentle in its behavior. Love does not boil with jealousy or envy. Love does not parade itself or brag on oneself and is not puffed up like a pair of bellows or a puffer fish. The manifestation of the spirituals should be with exceeding kindness and gentleness. It is the draw of the Divine love expressed in the spirituals which will lead to Christ. There is no room to brag or extoll what one has done because no one but the Holy Spirit is capable of pouring the love of the Father through the spirituals into someone's life. The spirituals should have the gentleness and comfort of Christ our shepherd seeking and caring for a lost lamb.

Love is not unseemly or rude or behaves indecently. Love does not allow one to seek their own interests. Love doesn't allow the provoking to sharpness or bitterness in the spirit. Love does not keep a ledger book of hurts and trespasses; love does not even think about those things. The operation of the spirituals should always be with grace not rudely or impinging on the character of someone. The Holy

Spirit is seeking to use those who are willing to be forgotten or moved to the background so the Lord may become near and dear to those who are touched with a spiritual. The world and those of the world fight against the things of God and it would be easy to allow words and actions to disrupt the flow of the Holy Spirit. Those who fight against God are often the ones who want and need God the most. They like Paul, do not realize their actions are not pleasing to the Lord even though they may believe what they do is right.

Love does not rejoice in unrighteousness but rejoices in the truth. The spirituals have the power to break the yokes of bondage which keep people enslaved. The truth and the reality of applied truth sets people free. Love desires to set those who are bound free to grow in the grace of our Lord. Not only does love not rejoice in unrighteousness but when we love we should have a great compassion to seek the best for others.

Love covers and protects; love believes in others; love sees the bright side and does not despair. Love endures; it perseveres as a good soldier. Love survives everything for God is love and He is eternal. The manifestation of the spirituals is an outward expression of the love of God. As such the spirituals should also characterize the love of God. Even though God's love is perfect it flows through human vessels so there is also the possibility the outworking of love is imperfect. However if we follow the guidelines of love which Paul wrote in this chapter there will be less of us and more of God in the expression of the spirituals.

When the Lord reigns in the millennial kingdom and in the age of ages there will be no need for the spirituals. That which is perfect does away with all things which are now just parts of the whole. Until that day we have a responsibility to desire and seek after the spirituals so the love of the Father and the Love of the Lord Jesus Christ will have an avenue of grace to reach into the lives of those who need what only the Lord may provide.

The spirituals function from the heart and love of God. We should love with His love and seek to show that love to others by desiring the spirituals and pursuing love. The heart of the Father is to reach and touch the world. He has chosen to reach out through imperfect human vessels. It is an honor and a humbling experience to be used by the

Holy Spirit to manifest the love of the Father and make a difference in someone's life.

Chapter Review

The spirituals should flow and operate with the agape love of God. Knowing the spirituals are a manifestation of God's love should serve to motivate us to desire the spirituals and have the love of the Father and our Lord flow through us.

Chapter Sixteen: But Ye Shall Receive Power...

Christ is quoted in the first chapter of Acts as saying "But you shall receive power when the Holy Spirit has come upon you: and you shall be witnesses to Me in Jerusalem, and in all Judea and Samaria and to the end of the earth." The word for power is dunamis. According to Strong's exhaustive concordance this is miracle working power; it is a mighty power. Throughout this book I have tried to show the truth about the Holy Spirit coming and the supernatural aspect of His ministry through the spirituals and the grace and privilege of praying in an unknown tongue and here is another truth to add to what has been shared. We receive power when the Holy Spirit comes upon us.

With great power the apostles gave witness and Stephen full of faith and power did great miracles. We know Christ did great miracles. Do we have the same power? Yes, we have the same Holy Spirit and the Holy Spirit is looking for willing vessels to yield to His leading. Paul's prayer in Ephesians one nineteen stated he wanted us to know, *"what is the exceeding greatness of His power toward us according to or using the exact same measure of the working of His mighty power"*.

How was this power received? It was received after the Holy Spirit came upon them. This is the pattern given in the Bible. I have not seen any other method God has chosen to enable His children with power. In Ephesians chapter three and verse sixteen Paul's prayer was for us to be strengthened with might in the inner man. We need the power of the Holy Spirit giving our spirit some *dunamis*. Again in Collossians we are strengthened with might. (Col. 1:11). In Romans Paul said mighty signs and wonders by the power of the Spirit of God was evident when he preached the gospel of Christ. In all these verses it is referring to the *dunamis* power or might from the Holy Spirit.

Paul wrote in First Thessalonians that the gospel was not in word only but in power and in the Holy Spirit. When he wrote the second epistle to Timothy he wrote this in Chapter one and verse seven. *"For God has not given us a spirit of fear, but of power and of love and of a sound mind."* Paul also wrote some would have a form of godliness but deny its power. God's power works for us, in us and through us. We need to have a revival of the Holy Spirit and power. The power flows through the body of Christ using human instruments. Will you be a part?

Eighteen of the twenty-seven books of the New Testament use a form of the word *dunamis*. The mighty power of the Lord is a part of our lives in the transforming miracles which happens when we accept the provision of Christ. The world is held together by the authority and power of Christ. The demonstration of the gospel is with *dunamis*, it is with the power of the spirituals.

The church started with the power and presence of the Holy Spirit on the Day of Pentecost. Why would we think we could receive power in any other way than the Biblical examples? The power of the Holy Spirit is not only for the manifestation of the spirituals but also to help in our daily growth, to help in overcoming the flesh, to help in understanding the Word of God and to help us know the heart and ways of the Lord.

In the King James Version the word power is the translation used for both *dunamis* and *exousia*, which in the New King James Version is translated authority. Understanding the power of the Holy Spirit is to also understand the authority which comes from the Word of God and the Holy Spirit. We need to understand the authority which Christ, through the scriptures, has given to the ecclesia. To manifest this authority we also need to rely upon the Holy Spirit for guidance, direction and understanding. We have authority over the enemy but we need to know how to exercise that authority. That knowledge comes from the Word of God and the Holy Spirit. Understanding the authority of the believer is vital but also more in depth than most realize.

When Christ sent the disciples to go before Him he gave them authority over unclean spirits and the authority to heal sickness and diseases and to tread on serpents. We have authority to claim the promises of the Bible. We are adopted into the family of God with authority and power to do what the Lord calls us to do.

I believe another aspect of understanding power and authority from the Holy Spirit comes from knowing the Holy Spirit is the earnest of our inheritance. It occurs three times in the King James New Testament and is translated guarantee in the New King James Version. The Greek word is *arrhabon* and according to Strong's Concordance has this meaning: "a pledge, part of the purchase money or property given in advance as security for the rest: -earnest." Earnest, according to Webster's Dictionary is the part given beforehand as a pledge for the whole. The concept is the Holy Spirit is our guarantee, He is our down payment of eternity and He is the pledge that God will fulfill all His promises to us.

2 Corinthians 1:22; *"who also has sealed us and given to us the Spirit in our hearts as a guarantee."* (NKJV) *"Who hath also sealed us, and given the earnest of the Spirit in our hearts."* (KJV)

2 Corinthians 5:5; *"Now He who has prepared us for this very thing is God, who also has given us the Spirit as a guarantee."* (NKJV) *"Now he that hath wrought us for the selfsame thing is God, who also hath given unto us the earnest of the Spirit."* (KJV)

Ephesians 1:13,14; *"In Him you also trusted after you heard the word of truth, the gospel of your salvation, in whom also, having believed you were sealed with the Holy Spirit of promise, who is the guarantee of our inheritance until the redemption of the purchases possession to the praise of His glory."* (NKJV) *"In whom ye also trusted after that ye heard the word of truth, the gospel of your salvation: in whom also after that ye believed were sealed with that Holy Spirit of promise, which is the earnest of our inheritance until the redemption of the purchased possession unto the praise of His glory."* (KJV)

Why do I believe this aspect of the Holy Spirit should be included in this chapter on power? The Holy Spirit is our earnest money; he is the escrow of our inheritance. He is the promise that as Christ was resurrected so shall we also be resurrected. But, it is much more than a mere promise that we belong to Christ. If I put a down payment on a house or car it is something very real and tangible. It is the same with the Holy Spirit. He not only abides with us, leads and guides us, bears witness with our spirits that we are the children of God, but also manifests Himself with power and authority in our lives.

Christianity is the only religion which not only has the promise of eternity but has a guarantee of eternity and the down payment or earnest of eternity for us to have in our lives until our journey on earth is over. The power and authority given because the Holy Spirit is our guarantee should cause rejoicing in our hearts and praise to flow from our lips. Just like the money we would put down to buy a house it is something real and without it the bank would not believe we were serious about purchasing the property. The Lord Jesus Christ was serious when He purchased us and has given the guarantee of our inheritance to us in the Holy Spirit.

Unlike money which a bank may put in a vault and may not be used, the Holy Spirit is our guarantee. He is the one who uses us and we have the full assurance of being adopted into the family of God every time we are used to witness, prophesy, when we have any of the spirituals flow through us and when we pray in our spiritual language. It is proof positive we are sealed for and unto the Lord. That is a powerful statement of ownership. We are adopted into the family of God and bestowed with the ability to function with the spirituals and continue the family legacy of loving others through the spirituals.

Chapter Review

We receive power after being baptized into the Holy Spirit. I have found no other way to receive this power than this teaching from the Word of God. The New Testament has many uses of the word power and authority. They confirm the baptism of the Holy Spirit.

Chapter Seventeen: The Church and
"The Church"

What comes to your mind when you hear something about the church? Do you think of the building where you and others gather to fellowship and to learn? Do you think of all the churches around the world? What do you know about the church? We tend to think of a church as a building where members gather to worship, learn and do the work of the ministry. The church in America is also a legal entity with certain rights and privileges. The word used in the Bible is ekklesia meaning those who are called out; a religious community. The church from a Biblical viewpoint is the people who have accepted and are following Jesus Christ. The church, or the body of Christ, should be the outward manifestation of God's love and His interaction with His children. Too often the church is fighting among itself. Differing viewpoints and not enough tolerance and acceptance show a poor example for the world to follow. The church is the only organization which kills the wounded among the fellowship. I sin, you sin and so does everybody else. Only one man ever lived a perfect life; He is our savior Jesus Christ. When someone fails in the church it becomes fodder for gossip. I believe the church will grow in grace so when a person fails that knowledge will never go outside the church walls or never leave the meeting place (if it doesn't happen to be a traditional church).

I believe two avenues are occurring and will continue until the Lord returns. One, there is a separation growing between the church as the *ekklesia* and the church as a religious or Christian institution. Those who want to sit and be entertained in a Christian atmosphere but are not willing to grow in the grace, gifts and callings will continue to be content as spectators. There is a growing surge of Christians who are not satisfied with the status quo but are seeking to live with the power and glory demonstrated in the book of Acts. They are seeking to know God, to really know God. They are not content to know about God but desire the presence, power and majesty of the King of Kings and Lord of Lords.

The structure of many churches tends to lead those attending to be spectators. The Word of God is as individual as it is corporate. What applies to a body also applies to an individual. We are all called of God for a purpose and it is His purpose. The church is to be a witness for Jesus. Does that mean only the activity of a corporate structure is legitimate or does it also mean that we as individuals must minister on a daily basis and not just inside a church building? Many churches want their members to be active but only within the parameters and oversight of the governing body of that church. Don't misunderstand what I am saying. A lot of churches are doing great things for the kingdom of God and are reaching out in their communities to make a difference. But, when the ministry is stifled under authority by those placed in that position individual growth suffers.

I am not saying to leave a church. Find where and how the Lord desires for you to minister. If it is within the confines of a local fellowship then serve with all your heart. We will answer to the Lord for what we do for him. Telling the Lord that the pastor or the board wouldn't let you do what Jesus called you to do might not be the best response when you are standing in His presence. If the Lord has called you then there will be a way to fulfill that calling. Our responsibility is to find that way. If you are called to teach your ministry may be on your job where you teach others the process and procedures. You may teach at a school. You may teach in a small group. You may teach at a Sunday school or Bible class but you will find a way to teach.

We are to be led by the Holy Spirit. We are to walk in the Spirit and not in the flesh. The greater our desire to please the Lord the more His grace works in and through our lives. That is one reason for the separation between the church and 'the church, the body of Christ'. Those who desire to be used and to please the Lord will receive a greater impartation of grace and power in these last days to make a difference in the world. Will you be a difference maker?

The second occurrence I believe is happening and will continue to surge forward is the return of many wounded saints to an active participation in the body of Christ. I believe this is a supernatural act of grace from the Holy Spirit to change the heart of the wounded. I believe they will again experience the hunger and desire for the things of the Lord. They will forgive and be healed. They will be encouraged by others and will seek a place to belong. The Holy Spirit will lead many to pray for the return of these wounded warriors to the battle for souls.

As the Holy Spirit is uniting believers to form the body of Christ many will wander from their established traditions to flow in the grace and sweetness of the Holy Spirit. At the same time there will be those who are not comfortable with the supernatural experiences. I think it is normal to have supernatural experiences. My Father is supernatural. He is the creator of the universe and everything in it and His Son holds all things together by His power. Being supernatural is part of the family legacy and without moving in the supernatural or the spiritual I would have to question if I was really part of the family.

Paul wrote an interesting verse in 1 Corinthians 14:38. *"But if anyone is ignorant, let him be ignorant."* If any choose to not learn and grow in understanding of the spiritual manifestations and the grace of God for those experiences let them be unlearned. I do not understand why anyone would choose to quench and grieve the Holy Spirit by not growing and seeking the spirituals with an intense passion and zeal. Christ would have been a great teacher without the spirituals but He was so much more when the Father's love was manifested by healing, by feeding the multitudes, by casting out tormenting spirits and by calming the storms.

Some will choose to not walk with the Holy Spirit's power and will miss many blessings not only for themselves but also for and to others. That is different than not wanting to know about the spirituals and being or staying unlearned. The results will be much the same. There will be a lack of power.

One last aspect of the church which has been changing and will continue to grow is in fellowship. Fellowship is not just socializing or just getting together for a meal though that may be a part of fellowshipping. That is one level of fellowship. Another is a spiritual occurrence where the focus is on allowing the Holy Spirit to lead the time together for mutual benefit, spiritual growth and to strengthen those who are fellowshipping. Many things occur when we fellowship. On a surface level friendships are formed and social activity meets the needs of the people. There may also be conversations which stir the mind and soul to a greater understanding of spiritual truth.

There is another deeper aspect to fellowship and occurs on a spiritual level; it takes place between the spirit of man and the spirit of man or woman. I was at a funeral home for the viewing of the father of a friend and was watching and feeling the interaction when guests would arrive to show respect and honor. I could see how her spirit responded when someone came through the door. Her spirit would respond to them before they said anything or gave a hug and condolences. I spent the afternoon watching, feeling and seeing what was a spiritual ministering from human spirit to human spirit.

One Sunday morning, at one of the lowest times of my life, during worship I was crying out to the Lord silently. "Lord I am empty and I have nothing to give to these people today." I wasn't asking for strength or for anything. I was stating my condition to the Lord. For some reason it didn't enter my mind to ask the Lord for help, I was broken and had nothing. A lady walked into service with her son who was in my martial arts class. I sensed she and her husband had a disagreement about her coming to church because it was not where they attended. I sensed she had a divine leading to be there. When she walked in my spirit was drawing strength from her spirit and her presence. What started when she walked in continued throughout the worship service and ministered strength and grace so I brought forth a sermon. I know my spirit received strength from her presence. I honestly believe if she hadn't walked in I would not have given the sermon. I needed to be ministered to on a spiritual level and the Lord provided someone to do that.

The gospels of Matthew, Mark, and Luke recount the events in Gethsemane. The Lord went to the garden with his disciple and instructed eight to remain back and took Peter, James and John to be closer to Him. He went a stones throw away and prayed. Three times He went back to the three and found them sleeping. An angel also came and strengthened Him. Why did the Lord need the three to be closer to Him in His hour of agony? I believe Jesus in His humanity needed to draw from the strength of their spirits to make it through the agony of His prayer until the angel strengthened Him. Their spirits were close to Him even while they were sleeping.

That is the type of fellowship the church is embracing. It also adds a dimension to the verse from Hebrews 10:25 which states; "...*not forsaking the assembling of ourselves together, as is the manner of some, but exhorting one another, and so much the more as you see the Day approaching.*" The words one another are not in the original text but were added. We are to assemble and exhort both with words and with our spirits.

I imagine most reading this will remember an experience when friends comforted us when we needed comforting. It is when we come together that our spirits and our words exhort another or maybe the whole assembly. There is an importance to meeting so our spirits minister to one another. Your spirit may have the spiritual strength someone needs and when you are not at a meeting there is much which is lost. That is fellowship at the deepest human spirit level and is a necessity as we see the time approaching for the Lord's return. We give one another strength and lift another's spirit by our presence.

I am passionate about prophecy and believe the church must continue to grow in the practice and use of prophecy. I am not sure how to explain this but I sense what is taking place in someone's spirit when they receive a prophecy. I may sense there is healing from spiritual wounds; I may sense an excitement or joy in their spirit and I may sense a comforting peace which calms the spirit. I know and sense that there is more power and grace to minister and transform lives through prophecy than I understand. I have seen and sensed the great love of the Father manifested through prophecies. If the church could understand what I have seen, sensed, and feel from those who receive a prophetic word to edify, exhort and or comfort the church would gain a passion and desire to prophesy which would change their world. May you walk in the Spirit and grow to have real fellowship with one another and with the Father, Son and Holy Spirit. Blessings to you.

Chapter Review

The church biblically is the followers of Christ, people regardless of where they meet. These followers are human and think and behave differently. Some are active and want to learn and connect with God. Others are spectators and are satisfied to sit back and not become involved. Many wounded believers are searching for a deeper spiritual understanding. They are experiencing God's supernatural powers. Fellowship is more than getting together for a meal and games and gossip. Our spirits connect with each other on a level that we may not understand. They can gain strength from others. We learned about this with Jesus in the Garden of Gethsemane.

Made in the USA
Monee, IL
14 October 2021